Printed in The United States of America

Cover, text design and art by Nima Veiseh

ISBN: 9781700165121

Library of Congress Control Number: 2019917009

Library of Congress Cataloging-in-Publication Data

Veiseh, Nima, author.

Markets with Memory / Nima Veiseh.

Includes bibliographical references.

ISBN 9781700165121

CONTENTS

Nima Veiseh

Dedication

This book is dedicated to my mom and dad. Without their belief in my dreams, I would never have been able to achieve what I have wanted to in life, nor to help bring science to a whole new frontier.

To my grandmother, too. I hope revolutionary new research advances in our field can help her to regain her memory, which I cherish so dearly.

FOREWORD

Excerpt from "The Blind Men and The Elephant" by John Godfrey Saxe, 1872.

"It was [the blind] men of Indostan
To learning much inclined,
Who went to see the Elephant
(Though all of them were blind),
That each by observation
Might satisfy his mind.

The First approached the Elephant,
And happening to fall
Against his broad and sturdy side,
At once began to bawl:
"God bless me!—but the Elephant
Is very like a wall!"

The Second, feeling of the tusk,
Cried: "Ho!—what have we here
So very round and smooth and sharp?
To me 't is mighty clear
This wonder of an Elephant
Is very like a spear!"

The Third approached the animal,
And happening to take
The squirming trunk within his hands,
Thus boldly up and spake:
"I see," quoth he, "the Elephant
Is very like a snake!"

The Fourth reached out his eager hand,
And felt about the knee.
"What most this wondrous beast is like
Is mighty plain," quoth he;
"'Tis clear enough the Elephant
Is very like a tree!"

And so these men of Indostan
Disputed loud and long,
Each in his own opinion
Exceeding stiff and strong,
Though each was partly in the right,
And all were in the wrong!"

PART 0: INTRODUCTION TO MARKETS WITH MEMORY

This book is the first data science book for the hemp and cannabis industry. It serves, in part, as an economics textbook. It also serves as a management practicum, executed via data science strategy.

What is so important about writing a data science and business strategy textbook centered around the hemp and cannabis industry?

1. <u>A Novel Business Case Study</u>: The hemp and cannabis industry is a unique opportunity for study because it is one of the first major industries to open overnight. Other industries have had to adapt or grow into the world of big data, while the cannabis economy is a rare, modern case where the market is changing from illicit to legal with billions of dollars of commerce being legitimized very suddenly, leaving many questions about what to do and how to respond. This alone makes the cannabis economy an important case study for data scientists and business leaders needing to react strategically to the changing fabric of how modern business is being done in the world of big data. This

will be a theme discussed throughout the book.

2.   <u>Creating Better Companies Everywhere</u>: Lessons from this book can be applied as a strategic guide to benefit business leaders, data scientists, and policy makers across any industry that is touched by the modern world of big data. It is a new toolkit that extends the economics and financial modeling of today.

3.   <u>Learning From The Past</u>: History is littered with moments in which the failure of managers to work with data scientists led to catastrophic consequences, including corporate bankruptcies, the collapse of nations, and the deaths of innocent people. We can learn from history in order to avoid repeating it.

4.   <u>Better Serving Today's Consumer</u>: Through the introduction of concepts such as *markets with memory, convolutional markets, the innovation cycle,* and *bounded analysis,* both managers and data scientists will gain a broader overview about how their work and mission is impacting the consumer directly, and how they can learn to work together to better serve their clients.

5.   <u>Creating a Common Data Science Language</u>: This is the first comprehensive survey of different factors and metrics affecting the Cannabis Economy, all of which I believe will make it easier to share ideas, promote commerce, and innovate across the industry. Have you asked yourself why the book starts with Part 0? Since this book is meant to bridge the understanding gap between data scientists and managers, the first thing managers should understand about data scientists is that they start counting at 0, not 1. Misunderstandings like this are equivalent to the type of errors that resulted in a multi-billion dollar Mars rover crashing into the planet because somebody was coding in the Metric system of units and someone else was speaking in the English system of units. Speaking the same data language means you won't be the people who crashed the rover.

6.   <u>Correcting The Errors Of History</u>: The hemp and cannabis industry is unique in that it has been plagued by miseducation and misinformation for the better part of a century. Much of this is known to be rooted in racism and inequality (Waxman, 2019). There are countless other opportunities, like scientific advancements and life saving medical treatments, that have also been delayed for reasons not rooted in the process of scientific truth. These errors have lead to social costs and disenfranchisement, the true total of which may never be known. It is our responsibility to understand the issues in this context, and to stand on the right side of history going forward— promoting equality of opportunity and justice for all.

I recommend the reader to go through the material in order to get the most of the book, since each chapter is foundational to the next. This book is also meant to serve as a reference guide, however, shedding light on different aspects of the data pipeline and supply chain of the cannabis economy. The Appendix and References are provided to enable efficient access to sections you'll use later as a reference or otherwise return to those more often that serve you in your mission.

The conversational tone of the book may feel unorthodox to some. My goal is to address and serve a wide audience, from university classrooms to kitchen counters to corporate boardrooms to computer science labs. It is meant to be conversational, and I appreciate your patience and engagement as we weave everything together.

The remainder of this book is structured into 4 main parts. Part 1 is about the origins and motivations behind the need for managers and data scientists to be able to work together. Starting in the past, we'll run through a brief survey of business and economic history, focusing on episodes when data scientists and managers failed to work together resulting in dire consequences. As Mark Twain has often been attributed as saying, "history doesn't repeat itself, but it often rhymes."

Part 2 introduces the idea of markets with memory, as well as many of the strategic concepts that need to be understood by both managers and data scientists so that they can work together on both descriptive and prescriptive solutions to their customer's needs. Part 3 starts our deep-dive into the many metrics and mathematical principles that touch the cannabis supply chain from seed-to-sale. It is a thorough, first-of-its-kind walkthrough of the origins, cultivation, harvest and sale of the cannabis plant, from the perspective of a data scientist. This is what we would call a descriptive survey. Part 4 is a walkthrough of current data science models, with explanations of each intended to make the technology behind the math more understandable for the reader. We'll also look at how these models can be implemented in your business or organization to help drive innovation.

Also, while most data science books take a theoretical approach, I will walk you through a practical, applied, context-driven approach. Using the market and data pipeline as a road map, I will introduce theoretical concepts along this road map to give you accessibility to these elements. I will also introduce the state-of-the-art data science techniques utilized. This book is also meant to be an economic history that provides a historical account of the evolution of economic markets (a rare opportunity in economic and technological history), as well as an overview and survey of state-of-the-art machine learning processes and computer technologies.

As previously stated, this book is intentionally in its first edition, because it is meant to be updated, revised, and grow with the institutional knowledge that grows within our industry. Some of what we say here will be adjusted, and some of the numbers will differentiate. However, this is a rare opportunity to capture and perform this study in this point of space and time for a couple of reasons.

First, the industry is not fully legalized yet. This book has been published before federal legalization in the United States, which means that certain issues that exist now will not exist in the future. For example, a lot of companies must operate as multi-state operators (MSOs), which means that they have to have separate entities within each state, because you're not allowed to perform interstate commerce. Starting with the Marihuana Tax Act of 1937 and reinforced by the Controlled Substances Act of 1970, marijuana federally is considered a Schedule 1 substance (Sacco, 2014).

Second, with the passing of the Farm Bill in December 2019, and with the US's largest trade partner, Canada, having legalized marijuana on October 17, 2018, there is strong speculation and pressure from policy makers and business leaders alike to fully legalize the plant. Currently, hemp extraction is federally legal, provided that plants do not exceed a concentration of more than .3% THC (Comer, 2018). So, the plant could be used primarily for biomass, which could affect a great number of industries we'll discuss. The full legalization of the cannabis extract (concentration levels greater than .3% THC) is really what's going to drive this industry forward.

The first half of the book may be easier to read for business leaders, and more murky for data scientists, and for the second half, vice versa. My recommendation is this—read with an eye toward understanding both sides. Bridging the gap in understanding between business and data is the ultimate goal.

PART 1: COLLAPSE AND UNDERSTANDING THE PAST, WHERE MANAGERS AND DATA SCIENTISTS FAILED TO HELP THE CONSUMER

"No matter how profitable a company gets, without serving the consumer, the consumers will leave and the company will die. It doesn't matter how mathematically efficient a data scientist is being, if they aren't focused on the factors that affect the consumer, the accuracy and precision of their models will decrease. It doesn't matter how powerful an institution gets, the moment they lose the trust of and are out of touch with their constituents and consumer, they will lose power. All are meant, either directly or indirectly, to serve the consumer."

Question: What do three Nobel Prize winners and a root canal have in common?

Answer: Together they underscore what happens when data scientists and managers don't work together to do what is best for the client. But more on that to come.

While the start of this chapter can seem like a bad pun, its answer is no joke. In fact, it can have grave consequences. History has many examples when data scientists and managers not working together resulted in catastrophic bankruptcies, economic recessions, and the collapse of nations.

Whether you are a business leader, data scientist or managing an institution, there is one thing that can always be agreed upon: the consumer must be served. Yes, businesses have profit incentives, data sciences are working on efficiencies, and institutions are always trying to get stronger. In the end, however, none can survive in the long run without serving the consumer.

No matter how profitable a company gets, without serving the consumer, the consumers will leave and the company will die. It doesn't matter how mathematically efficient a data scientist is being, if they aren't focused on the factors that affect the consumer, the accuracy and precision of their models will decrease. It doesn't matter how powerful an institution gets, the moment they lose the trust of and are out of touch with their constituents and consumer, they will lose power. All are meant, either directly or indirectly, to serve the consumer.

The Root Canal

"Where was all my data, and what was I paying for?"

In 2019, while in the course of writing this book, I experienced a health scare that resulted in multiple visits to various hospitals and medical centers. And by "various" I mean nine medical centers over a period of five business days, with multiple CAT scans, X-rays, and evaluations from different medical professionals. Despite having a well-paying job and what I believed was good health insurance, by the time I reached Friday, I discovered that I had spent nearly all of my savings trying to cover insurance co-pays and incidental costs related to my healthcare. I would later find out that this story is more common than I had known, with individuals going into great debt to cover their own or their loved one's healthcare needs.

By Friday, I had been told by medical professionals that the infection may have gotten into my bone and nerve tissue, and I would need a root canal to remove the infection residing there. When I arrived at the endodondist's office, I was told that there was inflammation and infection that may not have been resolved by my previous doctors. They said that without a 3D scan of my teeth, they would not be able to confidently know if or where they could administer anesthetics for the root canal without spreading the infection. I was told that my insurance would not cover the 3D scan and that I would need to pay out of pocket.

At this point, I couldn't afford an additional scan so I tried to think of alternatives and also asked what my options were. I asked if the previous doctor notes were stored somewhere that they could review. They said no. I asked, if they could call the doctor to get any insights. They said that they don't usually, but they would try -- only to find a dismissive response on the other end. I asked, what about the previous CAT Scans and X-rays that I had already received and paid for? They said that "everyone's system is different" and they could only trust the results from their own system.

I was left with only one choice. If I wanted to receive this root canal and clear this infection from my body— an infection that had caused nearly a week of fever, pain and lost productivity— I would need to sign a consent waiver to allow the doctor to perform the root canal without any anesthetic. After deliberation and mustering all of my courage, I consented. For your sake, I will spare you the rest of the details of that visit.

After leaving the office, I asked myself several important questions:

1. Where was all my data, and what was I paying for? I am able to store a decade of emails securely all in one place for free, but not my health history.

2. Why were none of my doctors using the previous data in my medical history to deepen their insights into my condition and help me? It seems like the more data available, the better it is for everyone, instead of repeating scans and redoing visits.

3. How is it possible that I could have spent my entire savings in just one week on healthcare expenses? I thought modern healthcare technology made care better and more affordable in many ways.

The short answer was that data scientists in the healthcare field were not working closely enough with decision makers and business leaders to address these solvable problems. The longer answer about why, comes next.

The Three Nobel Prize Winners

"How can a sustainable economic system built to heal consumers, actually unsustainably deprive the consumer of economic power?"

I realized that my economic model to help explain my experience, and the experience of countless others, has its foundations in the work of three Nobel Prize winners in the field of Economics. As far as Nobel Memorial Prize in Economic Science recipients go, these three can be considered a unique lot. This may explain why nobody until this book has appeared to connect the dots between them.

Elenor Ostrom is the first and only woman, as of the writing of this book, to win the prize. Her 2009 commendation came from her work on the *Theory of the Commons*, which addressed the challenges inherent in institutions managing public goods for society. She explored important questions like: when everyone is dumping pollutants in the same river, who do you charge a pollution tax to and how much (Ostrom, 1990)?

Daniel Kahneman is a psychology professor and the first non-economist by profession to win the prize. His 2002 prize was for *Prospect Theory*, which laid out the mathematics explaining how individuals make different, sometimes irrational decisions based on whether they see a situation from the perspective of perceived losses versus perceived gains, even if the outcomes have the exact same average expected value (Kahneman et al., 1979).

Paul Romer is an economist by training, but often chooses to utilize his toolkit as an economist to investigate other fields. He has acted as a professor in the business schools of both Stanford University and New York University, promoted the idea of charter cities in his TED talk, and according to a September 2019 New York Times article, even attended the Burning Man Arts Festival. His 2018 Nobel prize was for his work in *Endogenous Growth Theory*, in which he helped to explain how technological innovation and human skills factor into long term economic growth (Romer, 1990).

There are several important factors that tie together these pioneers in their fields, which will all lead to the theory we will continue to explore in the remainder of Part 1 and into Part 2. The overlap that the *Theory of the Commons, Prospect Theory,* and *Endogenous Growth Theory* have is encompassed in the following five points:

1.   **They are not stateless.** Unlike many economic theories or computer models, these models keep a *state* (a record or memory of the past) in order to know what to do next.

2.   **They consider the human factor.** Many models before that, even many major ones used for pricing something as human as a contract between two people, considered surprisingly few human elements to obtain accurate results.

3.   **They each consider how institutions affect their models.** Institutional Economics did not get significant coverage until the 1990s and early 2000's with the work of Douglass North and Daron Acemoglu. Institutional Economics deals largely with the idea that non-economic actors and policy makers, like government institutions, can play a role in affecting economic outcomes (Acemoglu et al., 2005).

4.   **They each considered the role of technology as a driving factor in their models.** Since the 1950s with the Nobel Prize-winning work of Robert Solow and Trevor Swan, computer technology was typically placed into the same category as forks and tractors, all considered *physical capital.* Later we would understand that physical capital has many technological levels that can give many different degrees of benefit to the user (Solow, 1956).

5.   **They benefited greatly from advances in data collection.** Advances in the variety and amount of data that can be collected in all parts of life, helped to validate all three of these theories.

What these theories do not individually explain is the following: How can a sustainable economic system built to heal consumers, actually unsustainably deprive the consumer of economic power? In other words, how did we get to a point where the apparently competitive market could suck a consumer dry of their wealth? Or, what is the economic explanation for how a healthcare system that bankrupts its consumers stays in business, and how did we get here in the first place? It seems impossible that there be a sustainable business model where you bankrupt you consumers, right? How is greed sustainable in an economic system in such a way that it goes unchecked by all other parts of the free market? It would seem that you would shrink your consumer base and market share until you run out of those willing and/or able to pay for your service.

This is what my post-root canal self was wondering, and these musings were the origins of what we will explore in the coming sections— the Theory of Markets with Memory, or will be later known as Convolutional Market Theory.

A Brief Economic History of Greed

"In the 20th Century, we watched as greed evolved into internal managerial malpractice."

Throughout history, we have seen greed take many forms. You do not need to know yet what Convolutional Theory is in order to understand the rest of this section. Just know that this section illustrates what happens when a Convolutional Market is broken, which is most often a result of decision makers and data scientists not effectively working together. Throughout human history, the forms of greed and theft have evolved to survive, but the underlying principle has always remained the same: using non-economic factors to deprive someone else of economic power.

At the earliest times in human history, before the Middle Ages, greed and the stealing of economic power were largely done by force, and sheer physical power. An invading party would walk into a bakery or bank, and demand all of the money or else face the risk of being murdered. Historically, it would manifest as as outright bank robbery, or else through outright dishonesty via the breaking of a handshake agreement or contract. What did greed look like then? It was the physically strong stealing from the weak.

Then, after the Middle Ages, we found ourselves in the Italian Renaissance of the 15th and 16th centuries. The Medicis, along with other famous italian banking families, invented and promoted the double-entry bookkeeping accounting system we still use today, which in a way made it harder to cheat or distort transactions. Additionally, the invention of the printing press allowed for the dissemination of multiple copies of contracts and transactions ("A Revolutionary Treatise", 2019).

So what did robbery look like then? It most often took the form of the economically and politically privileged using their power of administration to control the books, build walls around their wealth, and distort transactions in their favor. It is a lack of accountability. This is one of the earliest examples of what happens when business leaders choose not to listen to the numbers, positioning themselves instead as both the decision maker and data manager. Decision making power was never checked by the reality of measurements and numbers, and seldom by even public institutions like the courts. Shakespeare's *Merchant of Venice* satirized this issue all the way back in 1605 (Shakespeare & Cone, 1900). What did greed look like then? It was the educated and entitled stealing from the uneducated and disenfranchised.

By the 18th and 19th centuries, we begin to see governments and corporations working more closely together via industrialization and democratization. This was due, in large part, to at least two reasons. First, industrialization and innovation meant that private citizens could now be major drivers of the economy. Second, democratization meant that private citizens now had a voice in governance. Government institutions by the people and for the people would more often work with people to accomplish public interests -- like building a Transcontinental Railroad. Now, not only was there more transparency, but also people had a say in what was going on. What did greed look like then? It was the connected stealing from the unconnected. It took the form of large contracts being handed to individuals based on administration and social connections -- not on the analytics, merit, or data available about who would perform the best job.

In the 20th century, we watched as greed evolved into internal managerial malpractice. What did greed look like then? It was the implanted administrators stealing directly from the unimplanted. The CEOs and executives inside of the company stealing from the inside. The executives of Enron leveraging the retirement assets of its own employees to prop up its value—lying about the numbers while also not hearing the warnings of those who understood what the data was saying (Swartz et al., 2004).

Another example of this problematic archetype comes to us through the Chernobyl Disaster. Scientists responsible for the data were ignored by those committing managerial malpractice. *Bounded analysis* was dishonestly handled: they reported that the full measurement was 3.6 roentgen of radiation, not because that was the actual reading, but that was the highest reading possible for the machine available on site (more on *bounded analysis* in Part 2). In a 2006 interview, Mr Gorbachev said: "The nuclear meltdown at Chernobyl 20 years ago this month, even more than my launch of Perestroika, was perhaps the real cause of the collapse of the Soviet Union five years later (The Economist, 2016)."

We see yet another iteration of this in the Great Recession of 2008, during which time theft took the form of administered contracts that appeared legitimate in the short-run but that data models said would fail in the long-run. Financial crimes like the ponzi scheme perpetrated by Bernie Madoff during that time are similar in structure ("The Madoff Case", 2009).

Legitimized Complexity: What happens when data scientists and

managers do not work together in a Convolutional Market

"[Greed] is now largely buried in complexity and systems, through administration costs and overhead."

Greed doesn't have to be intentional or malicious, it can be just a function of "trying to do your job right" or maximizing your teams value. What's more, we may not even realize we're doing it at our local level, until we see systemic collapse, either in the form of the bankrupting of private institutions (Enron and WorldCom crisis), the recessions within economics (2008 financial crisis), or the collapse of forms of governments (Chernobyl).

Going into the 21st Century: now that banks are secured by armed guards, government contracts are subject to more transparency, and corporations are subject to stricter monitoring, what form does greed take? And where could it possibly be so legitimized that nobody has done anything about it? How is accountability being distorted?

The answer is that greed is now largely buried in complexity and systems, through administration costs and overhead. Nickel-and-diming at the macro level, individual hedge fund managers that take 20% of the whole funds profits untaxed, or insurance companies creating layers of costs they recoup from -- all of this falls under the heading of modern greed, and modern greed takes the form of *legitimized complexity*.

Legitimized complexity happens when data scientists and decision makers do not work together. The entire job of a data scientist is to create transparency and simplify. Their work is typically to produce a model, representing a part of reality that can be abstracted to feel almost like a toy, so that we can play with it, and try to gain some very specific insight, given a certain amount of assumptions we consider acceptable. Data science is

17

the opposite of complexity, it takes complex systems and over-simplifies them. One of my favorite sayings in data science is that, "all models are wrong, but some are useful". All models are wrong because they are a simplification of reality, but that does not mean they cannot help explain a part of a complex phenomena.

Data science is a weapon that can either by used to serve the consumer, or hijacked to serve an individual through greed. In one case, data scientists and decision makers work together to find authentic avenues for better serving the consumer. In the other case, decision makers intentionally ignore the data scientists, the math and the numbers, and choose complexity and personal profit over the consumer they are meant to serve. Theoretically, the data scientists can also be weaponized to distort numbers, but at that point, they are no longer trying to discover through data and simplification, but rather to make the discovery of crimes more difficult through obfuscation and complexity. In summary, the will and the desires of the decision makers has taken priority over serving the consumer, resulting in increased complexity, not simplification.

How does all of this explain the unsustainable cost of our healthcare system?

I observe two types of legitimized complexity that impact the cost of healthcare. The first addresses the cost of physical capital, which relates to the costs of data and medical tests. The second deals with the cost of human capital, which addresses the cost of the doctors and medical professionals that provide care.

With what we now know, I now go back to my original three questions:

1.   **Where was all my data, and what was I paying for?** The answer was that is was all stored in different places, and we have a system of institutions that are responsible

for making it difficult to get to it. In other words, it's buried in administrative complexity. Yes, it is important to be HIPAA Compliant to protect medical data, since it is very sensitive personal information. However, the data is typically stored in such a way that it can't be easily accessed by those who need to, and I had to jump through hoops to figure out how to get it shared. Every opportunity where I could be blocked or inhibited, I was. The administration costs prevented me from accessing my own data and physical capital I had already paid for: CAT scans and X-rays. There were walls around my data engineered by those who seemingly had an interest in me having a hard time getting to my data. It felt like Renaissance Italy, and I was being asked for a pound of flesh by the Merchant of Venice.

2.   **Why were none of my doctors using my previous data about my medical history to deepen their insights into my condition and help me?** Because they didn't need to. If I disagreed with the doctor or the way they handled the situation, I was reminded of two facts. First, that it is in the doctor's interest to keep ordering tests in their own medical center, because it means they don't need to learn to read another system and it may even feed into their own revenue. Second, I had few choices for other doctors because there are just fewer doctors in the United States. In fact, through historically well documented practices of legitimized complexity, and American Medical Association has successfully kept the number of doctors produced every year in the US to a staggeringly low 26 per 10,000, as of 2016 (Worldbank.org, 2018). This is nearly half of every other first world country. Decision makers at the AMA have ignored the economics and data science, and continue to not promote the creation of new medical schools in a way that keeps up with the growth of the United States it serves -- thus keeping human capital at an artificially low level,

driving up prices. I couldn't go find another doctor if I wanted to, at least not before my infection got worse or I spiked a fever.

3.   **How is it possible that I could have spent my entire savings in just one week on healthcare expenses?** Administrative complexity. The first point emphasizes the burden of receiving the same test many times. The second point emphasizes the burden of doctor costs. But even after all of these, the administration of healthcare fees and costs is well calculated to dry up any remaining economic power from the consumer. Mismatched co-pays appear to strategically cover some parts of care, while ignoring other necessary parts of care. For example, my root canal, which was performed into my tooth to clear an infection and lower my fever, was partially covered. The crown required to protect the tooth after the root canal, however, was not covered by insurance. If you were a data scientist looking at the whole process, your model for healing your consumer would include the entire process— a root canal cannot technically be considered complete without sealing the area, otherwise you leave it exposed to reinfection. This is the equivalent of an insurance company paying for someone's brain surgery, but once the doctor was done cutting into the brain, forcing the patient to pay to have their skull put back together and stitched back up. Your brain was healed... the rest is your responsibility.

The answer to my three questions was simple: this is what happens when a market is hijacked in such a way that it serves the providers and not the consumers. Data is the ear and mouthpiece of the consumer and, at all stages, the data and the opportunity for data scientists to provide clarity was intentionally inhibited. The providers inhibited me from easily getting my data. The AMA (against the advice of economic theory and data analysis) keeps the supply of doctors low, making choosing between doctors less transparent and keeping costs high. Lastly, health care executives have strategically priced different elements of the healthcare process to acquire as much revenue as possible from the consumer, instead of finding ways to maximize their service to their clients by internalizing the preferences of the consumer.

How to move forward, as explained by Three Nobel Prize Winners and the Theory of Convolutional Markets

"Greed is what happens when the preferences of the producer are internalized by the market. When Convolutional Markets are working properly, the preferences of the consumer are being fully internalized by the market."

The fact pattern we see here is defined by the following two stylized facts. First, greed is a form of market inefficiency or tax where the preferences of the producer or decision maker, not the consumer, is internalized by a market. Second, preventing greed from establishing itself in a market means we need data to reach decision makers in the most liquid way possible, and we need those lessons and data to be internalized by the entire system as quickly as possible in order to keep costs low, make sure frictions don't rise, and maintain economic growth.

Greed is what happens when the preferences of the producer are internalized by the market. When Convolutional Markets are working properly, the preferences of the consumer are being fully internalized by the market.

Since the doctors were being prevented from using my data, they were not advancing their skills to help me in any special way. Romer's endogenous growth model would imply that this healthcare system is at a suboptimal growth level. When I asked myself then what can be done to help encourage doctors to help more, there was little I could do to incentivize them, as Ostrom's model would say that limited public resources, the management of which is not subject to market forces will lead to inefficiencies in doctors administration, as well as the use of my data. Then Kahneman's model, would help us understand that the high transaction costs are a result of the increased friction of the information of the commons. Greed attacks what first? Institutions. Institutions are the artificial memory of economic systems -- they set the tone for progress (Veiseh, 2010). This is true of every level of economics. From tariffs (making it illegal makes it harder to tax or tariff it), down to health care systems, down to social justice issues within the cannabis market.

Gordon Gekko said "greed is good" and this isn't a book that speaks against self-interest and free market principles. When institutions are used to overpolice an economy providing illogical tariffs (Trump/Hoover), layers of administration that lead to unqualified transactions (subprime loans), layers of paperwork that can allow for contract manipulation (Enron), or layers of checks against those who have the information to act (Chernobyl) — we observe instability. What often happens is that greed finds its way into institutions; as a result, the market is not able to perform a check on what is transpiring, and the institutions become the memory instead of the economy itself, which is how it ideally should be.

We are at a rare time in history where we have the opportunity to watch all three of these actors figure out their missions, and come into the world of data science together. That is why a modern study of all three requires us to use a novel case study like the hemp and cannabis industry. This book is about how we can manage those unsustainable taxes and deadweight losses from our system, by having decision makers and managers working together with the fact finders. That's what institutions are: the place where decisions makers work together with scientific fact finders. Science is the mouthpiece of the data world around us.

Institutions distort the ability of the free market to be measured. Which is ok, to a small degree. We know that we need to police a bit; however, when the policy within institutions leaves the hands of those institutions and become influenced by the interest *being policed*, it is then that you see a collapse. Greed is what happens when anything except the interest and utility of the consumer is internalized within an economic system.

That's why when all three elements here are working together in balance, prices almost always fall across the board. Production gets cheaper at every stage of the system, and value is allowed to be generated everywhere.

PART 2: STABILITY AND UNDERSTANDING THE PRESENT: HOW DO CONVOLUTIONAL MARKETS HELP MANAGERS AND DATA SCIENTISTS BETTER SERVE THE CONSUMER?

"The legalization of the cannabis industry across global markets of all sizes marks a paradigm shift in businesses, because it is occurring after the advent of big data."

Now that we have an idea for how Convolutional Markets have broken down in the past and learned from the lessons of history, we have the opportunity to get them to work in creating value for the consumer. The rest of this book is how through a Theory of Convolution Markets, we can get Decisions Makers and Data Scientists (DMADS) to work together to best serve the consumer.

This book, crafted for everyone ranging from CEOs and C-level executives of companies to consumers and the cultivators in between, is meant to provide a scientific approach to business strategy, and provide education about the hemp and cannabis industry— an industry plagued by misinformation and miseducation for the better part of a century. The goal of this text is to examine the nature of the emerging cannabis and hemp market (hereafter known as the "cannabis economy") and the inputs affecting its related products. While this book is not specifically or entirely about the hemp and cannabis industry, it is the primary case study. Data science requires us to recognize that even the best idea and concept in the world is "dead in the water" if you do not have a clearly defined framework for understanding the concepts, vocabulary, units of measure, and values properly and consistently communicated. The appendix of this book contains a list of these concepts. This is an economics textbook that is the first edition of many anticipated editions that will document the physical evolution and economic history of the hemp and cannabis industry.

Understanding the Gap Between Decision Makers and Data Scientists

"A manager's ability to convey requirements and manage expectations effectively depends on the ability of a data scientist to help those managers understand what is required to get the job done."

In my experience working as a data scientist in close proximity to decision-making executives, one constant I have noticed presents in the inevitable adoption of big data strategies. Successful companies must bridge the notable disconnect between decision making by leadership and information available to and created by data scientists. A manager's ability to convey requirements and manage expectations effectively depends on the ability of a data scientist to help those managers understand what is required to get the job done.

One source of conflict is the perceived cost and value of time investment needed to do this effectively. This is primarily because there are conflicting incentives for both. Executives seek a quick turnaround because they are under pressure to meet the bottom line. In contrast, data scientists understand that there's a whole process of development that needs to be done prior to making decisions. This book seeks to provide an intersection between the two and, in turn, a better method of strategic thinking for managers and data scientists. This new strategic thinking will allow DMADS to work together and be more fully informed about each other's roles, internalizing how they can strategically work together to create more efficient outcomes and stronger results within the data scientist team while also satisfying the executives' requirements.

Why this dichotomy exists can be actually very easily seen by looking at the two primary paradigms that are utilized by managers and data scientists (and developers) in general. Developers primarily, if you look at their development schedule, use a type of recently popular development methodology called *agile* (Highsmith & Cockburn, 2001), driven by the idea that development in an innovative space, which is traditionally being used in the space of computer technology, can be done in a series of "sprints" that can last anywhere between a couple of days to a couple of weeks. A minimum viable product is developed in intervals and then incrementally developed, such that you have a proof of concept that can then be scaled.

If you look at the foundations of *agile development*, you'll notice something fundamental to the engineering field (Beck & Kent, 2006). When a descriptor is used for a particular sprint, the traditional format might be to say, "**who** is the stakeholder? What do they want and why?" A storyline in an agile sprint, however, is typically structured as a blank, which could be a client or customer or developer, e.g. "*I want blank*" (let's say a more efficient light bulb), so that I can save money on my energy bill. This statement from the engineer's perspective communicates value in a straightforward way. Conversely, however, if looking at the paradigms proposed by management experts like Simon Sinek, the typical approach is to start with the *why* (Sinek, 2009). The order of operation from Sinek's perspective is *why*, then *how*, then *what*. The dichotomy between these two paradigms of thought is a very clear indicator of how and why conflict exists between managers and data scientists (Abrahamsson et al., 2002).

Managers and Data Scientists Strategically Working Together

"Most managers do not realize that data science is more similar to science than engineering."

What is another aspect of data science that managers often do not understand? The necessary requisites that come up in the course of creating a data science infrastructure. As a manager, it is very important to understand that creating a data oriented infrastructure takes time and investment. Of course, like any research endeavor, there has to be investment upfront and trial and error before innovation occurs. In fact, what most managers, in my experience, may not seem to understand (and what many people just getting into the field of data science don't seem to understand) is that the vast majority of data science actually involves the cleaning (the term is *munging*) of data because in computer science (as we like to say) if you put garbage data in, you get garbage data out.

What's more, most managers do not realize that data science is more similar to science than engineering. With engineering you see the results right away; in science, you have to wait until the entire experiment plays out in order to observe the outcome. Data science is a more tempered version of RandD (not strictly engineering).

Thus, it is important for managers to understand how important it is to invest up front in this data infrastructure and provide proper lead time. It could take anywhere from 3 to 24 months, to build a proper data infrastructure, and it may be necessary to create an environment where you can collect data, clean the data, and extract insights from it.

And what is it then that data scientists don't understand? Many data scientists have said they are wary of visualization because it can dumb down their work and cause executives to draw conclusions that belie the nuance and uncertainty that is inherent in any scientific analysis (Berinato, 2019). In the rush to grab in-demand data scientists, however, organizations have been hiring the most technically oriented people they can find, but not considering whether they have the ability or desire to communicate with a lay audience. That would be fine... if those organizations also hired other people to close the gap. They typically don't. Organizations, instead, expect data scientists to wrangle data, analyze it in the context of knowing the business and its strategy, make charts, and present them to a lay audience.

That's unreasonable. That's a unicorn fantasy. Many efforts by data scientists fall short when it comes time to explain their results to decision makers. Narrative is an extremely powerful human contrivance and one of the most underutilized in data science. The ability to present data insights as a story will, more than anything else, help close the communication gap between algorithms and executives. And yet, "storytelling with data," a tired buzz phrase, is widely misunderstood. It is decidedly not about turning presenters into Stephen Kings or Tom Clancys. Rather, it's about understanding the structure and mechanics of narrative and applying them to dataviz and presentations. A favorite joke of mine about the industry is that "Machine Learning is done in Python, but Artificial Intelligence is done in PowerPoint." The presentation of data science to lay audiences —the ancient "last mile"—hasn't evolved as rapidly or as fully as the science's technical part. It must catch up. That means rethinking how data science teams are put together, how they are managed, and who is involved at every step through the process, from the first data stream to the final chart shown to the board. Until data scientists and companies can successfully traverse that "last mile", data science teams will underdeliver. They will provide, in Willard Brinton's words, foundations without cathedrals (Brinton, 1914).

What is Different about Integrating Data Science into the Cannabis Industry?

By reading this first data science textbook for an emerging data-driven industry (that has yet to be widely labeled as such), you are ahead of those who will inevitably need to adapt. Historically, industries emerged locally and grew in the absence of global data. Large companies were built before data science became a prevalent driver of everything within that industry.

The legalization of the cannabis industry across global markets of all sizes marks a paradigm shift in businesses, because it is occurring after the advent of big data, which we can set at around 2010. At that time, the big data era developed due to a confluence of key factors. First, cloud computing enabled large datasets to be stored and processed. Second, new opportunities for collecting data became available.

Today everything from your social media profiles to your search history are tracked by marketing analyst algorithms (Zikopoulos & Eaton, 2011). Your smart phone enables tracking of your location, what you consume, and how you consume it (Fawcett & Buhle, 1995). On the other end, consumers are able to directly respond to their needs by giving direct feedback to the company. This is a brand new era for data (Zhou et al., 2010).

Third, there have been massive increases in computing power and the ability to perform processing, which has enabled machine learning and artificial intelligence to take hold. For example, the nature of graphic processing units (GPUs) as developed primarily by NVIDIA has enabled more complex computations than ever before. Simply put, NVIDIA has been the industry leader. They discovered that these GPUs are able to not only perform graphics calculations but are actually very well specialized in performing very important and complicated numerical calculations, numerical optimizations, and prime number factorizations.

What is a 'Market with Memory'?

"A market with memory is an opportunity for data to be helpful to everyone in real-time."

A *market with memory* is a broad term that I am introducing as a concept for industries and how they will be affected by the introduction of big data within their industrial goals. The important point to understand about markets with memory (as opposed to regular markets within an equilibrium of traditional economics) is that, in traditional economics, there is this idea of supply intersecting with demand, which creates some equilibrium that establishes a price within that market. Typically, those forces are largely considered independent and not having any trajectory, or state (Baye, 2014).

However, a market with memory is an opportunity for data to be helpful to everyone in an industry in real-time. It is where a consumer observes a better outcome, because different parts of the supply chain along that market, through the advent of big data and the ability to remember how different elements, inputs and outputs, factor favorably into different parts of the process of satisfying the consumer. In a very broad sense, today you have markets with memories but in a non-standardized way.

For example, imagine you have a cultivator that tests one crop, experiments with the water levels given to the plant, and discovers that the plant didn't respond well on the first harvest. In response, they change the water levels for the next harvest and discover that the plant generated higher yields. The ability to remember the output of the previous yield allows one section of the market to adjust and pivot towards greater efficiency. The cultivator is able to optimize based on data collected. The time required for this improvement in the crop yield, between the different crop harvests, based on the change of inputs, we refer to as the "length of the innovation cycle." This is a concept that will be reviewed in context with convolutional markets later in this Section.

What is Changing about the Innovation Cycle?

The "innovation cycle" has largely been defined as a continuous cycle of product discovery, development, and commercialization that enables companies to keep reinvesting in the next generation of technology. It is considered to be the amount of time between incremental amounts of innovation, within a product or industry. For example, traditionally in the automobile industry, if we wanted to make improvements to a car (or any other widget), it would first have to be designed, and then the unique parts would have to be created for it. The whole car would be manufactured and finally sold to a consumer. That consumer would need to drive that car anywhere between one and 500,000 miles until it broke. Once the car broke, we would be able to disassemble it and find out why it broke. Then we would make necessary improvements for the next innovation cycle of parts and cars.

As you may notice in the above example, the length of the innovation cycle is actually 1.0, which is the entire length of the lifecycle of the car. This is true across many industries. In fact, if you look at the innovation cycles across some industries, it will tell you a lot about how quickly innovation is able to happen within those spaces. For example, in medicine, it's been documented that vaccines (despite the fact that humans have been practicing medicine for thousands of years) have only emerged in the last couple of centuries. Why might this be the case and what has happened since?

This happens to be the case because typically, until a person dies and has fulfilled their entire lifecycle, you couldn't traditionally just open them up and look inside. That is why inventions like the ability to disinfect and sanitize, to open the body and close it again, were amongst Nobel Prize winning inventions. The MRI, which enables us to see inside the living body to better understand internal events that might be affecting a person's health, has proven to be an important tool. The advent of technology and progress of technology in every field helps to shorten and tighten the innovation cycle.

It is critical for both managers and data scientists to understand the innovation cycles within their industry. In the context of managers, they are better able to strategically plan for industries (even those that rapidly change) by understanding the innovation cycles, how long they'll have to wait, and over what type of investment horizons they can promise innovation to increase their competitive advantage. For data scientists, this is just as important, because it helps them to understand how they should be aware of timeframe (as trends versus cycles) to better understand patterns and effects that might be impacting

Markets with Memory

a market. In both contexts, whether manager or data scientist, having an understanding of the macro scope and the problem's boundaries can create deeper insights and lead to better decision making.

What is a Convolutional Market?

"In a convolutional market, the tastes of the consumer are internalized within the market."

Introduced anecdotally in Part 1, a *convolutional market* is a brand new phenomenon in economics based on my academic research over the last decade and advances in big data analysis. The idea of a convolutional market diverges from our understanding of traditional economics, i.e. that a competitive price equilibrium (or the price that you end up paying at the store), is the result of some sort of equilibrium between supply and demand. Demand is largely a function of a consumer and their tastes. However, the market itself doesn't pivot or react to the person's taste. It only does so in the consumer's demand, by increasing supply in a particular way.

However, in a convolutional market, the tastes of the consumer are internalized within the market. The consumer not only affects demand, but also at the same time (through big data analysis and through the fact that the market has a memory along every part of the supply chain), may actually condense the length of the innovation cycle, as previously suggested. The consumer also affects the supply curve, as well, in real time.

How does this affect the innovation cycle and how do they relate? In the cannabis market, looking at a data process in a data pipeline from seed to sale, there is limited opportunity to implement big data across the industry (as it is being deregulated, and brought into the public eye). The U.S. government is actively working to create a system to track the inputs of products as hemp and cannabis are consumed.

33

There's an opportunity to change. To be able to track the inputs along every part of the supply chain, as mandated from the very onset of this industry, with everyone involved who touches the product (which has traditionally been a Schedule 1 substance). From the moment a seed is planted, to all of the inputs (i.e. water, light and soil nutrients), through cultivation, harvesting, extracting, delivery of product, and even further down the pipeline to retailer and consumer. All of these areas and stages within the supply chain have memory.

In traditional market economics, in a competitive supply equilibrium, there could only be one point at which the consumer affects the market, and that's at the point of sale or in the retailer space. In today's market, according to Henry and Finkelstein this is the frontier of where data is most prevalent in the hemp and cannabis industry (Hudak, 2018). From here on, we'll just call it the "industry."

We can expect waves of new efficiency and increased speed of innovation moving into the future with all of the increased volume of data that consumers are communicating and that the market is internalizing. Consider this: a particular strain is grown with a certain amount of water and light, then harvested and packaged into a distillate (these cycles can take anywhere between three and four months). After the consumer receives and tries the product from the retailer, they have the opportunity to give feedback on the product directly through an app to the wholesaler, retailer, or even the seed manufacturer, or through any number of data platforms, like New Frontier Data, Headset, Leafly or WeedMaps.

People can consume the product and identify the exact strain in a particular batch because it's been monitored from seed-to-sale. It can be reviewed on a website, discussed through a chat bot, or even identified by its serial number on the product. It is now fully traceable. Data points and insights collected can be communicated to key stakeholders throughout the supply chain, all adapting in real time to consumer preferences.

This idea of a convolutional market, therefore, is one in which a consumer's tastes can have an impact and actually permanently alter the structure of an industry. This can be done because the market remembers what the consumer preferred (based on direct consumer feedback), and takes into consideration that they are not just voting with their dollars but also stating their preferences and describing their experience. This means that consumer feedback evolves from simple "Yes or No" to asking "How and Why". Questions about first order effects ("Yes or No") can create opportunities to understand second order effects ("How and Why"). Ultimately, it creates an effect across the supply chain, whereby the market internalizes these adjustments in real time to create or maintain demand for the product.

The ability of the market to evolve quickly was echoed by Bruce Linton, the CEO of Canopy Growth, when, at the 2019 Cannabis Congress in NYC, he joked that his company is basically driving a car 100 miles an hour and swerving sideways perfectly into a parking spot between two cars with confidence. He understands he can do that— if one player in the industry is this agile, every player will need to adopt similar strategies to compete.

The Power of Uniting Data Scientists and Managers

"This book is designed to place the hemp and cannabis industry at the head of a new age in data-driven acceleration of the innovation cycle – a historical evolution."

The Cannabis industry provides a rare economic case study and a rare opportunity to watch a billion-dollar market effectively open overnight. The most recent, similar examples were perhaps 100 years ago in the removal of alcohol prohibition, and even more recently when computer scientist Tim Berners-Lee invented the World Wide Web (Mowery & Simcoe, 2002). While it's often confused with the Internet itself, the web is actually just the most common means of accessing data online in the form of websites and hyperlinks. The web helped popularize the Internet among the public, and served as a crucial step in developing the vast trove of information that most of us now access on a daily basis. This book is designed to place the hemp and cannabis industry at the head of a new age in data-driven acceleration of the innovation cycle – a historical evolution.

Creating a Common Mathematical Language in the Cannabis Industry

A high-level goal of this book is to provide an overview of the vocabulary, and understanding of the pieces, involved in the industry, such that both data scientists and managers can participate in an educated and positive way with all stakeholders. This book is also a rare opportunity to look at this industry in its nascency. This reference can provide a guide to regulators as a standardization of the language and nomenclature that has largely been undecided in such a fragmented industry. No matter what part of the industry you focus on, you will likely have an affect on some other part of the industry, at large.

A common mathematical language between cultivators working in similar roles is important. For example, whether you are cultivating worms as fertilizer to help feed plants, or whether you are an expert in extraction with ethanol, speaking the same language is important in communicating and receiving ideas that help you do your job better. If you're a manager working in the industry, it is helpful to understand other parts of the process, because they feed into your operational efficiencies and business outcomes.

A common mathematical language between those in different roles in the industry, like between cultivators and financial experts, is just as important. For example, the irrigation method a cultivator uses for their product will affect how much water gets consumed and utilized within the final product as it gets harvested. Understanding the data in the water management system will then affect downstream yields, the drying process, and the necessary technologies required for later extraction. This affects not only the cost of inputs, but the ability to project revenue. You need to have different considerations and factors that play into your strategic decision-making, in addition to the tactical approaches that are best for executing your business goals.

This book is ultimately to prepare you with an introductory framework for looking at each stage of the data-driven industry from an analytical perspective, which will serve you no matter whether you are a business leader, finance person or a cultivator. Context plus theory equals innovation. This book establishes a context for each stage of the pipeline at the beginning of Part 3.

This book will also give managers, and all people within the industry, a context of the different tools within data science that apply to different parts of this, and what their opportunities are within different stages of this pipeline. The "pipeline" I referred to (and will continue to refer to) is the pipeline from seed-to-sale that cycles back and is driven and measured by data. Because, as Lord Byron said, *what gets measured gets done*.

Speaking the same scientific language within the industry has positive consequences for those outside of the immediate cultivation process, like with ancillary services. This book also is to take an academic approach to a role that has not yet taken academic rigor to an industry, to have very important economic and medical impacts to our world within our lifetime.

Nima Veiseh

Understanding Bounded Analysis

In a space where science is very complicated, and quantitative analysis can yield many different results, there's a concept that is going to help both data scientists and managers who walk into an industry that has no precedent, sparse academic literature, and no context. That can be very daunting. One of the concepts I will introduce in this book for assisting executives and data scientists alike in managing, optimizing and executing on strategic processes to help enhance their business, in a place where the numbers may be unfamiliar. The concept is called *bounded analysis*.

Bounded analysis is a new business strategic concept, which involves reducing the data and its scope to two different levels of detail rather than trying to understand the entire universe of data and entire scope of different possibilities.

1.　　　　The first level of detail are the broad levers that are involved within the industry that might be driving the consumer experience. So in the context of the hemp and cannabis industry, candidate levers may be everything from the genetic makeup of the seed that is used to the soil inputs and nutrient inputs, to the light and water inputs, to the type of harvesting schedule that was utilized, or the amount of time that was taken to allow for growth. And then also looking at the type of equipment that was used for extraction, all the way through to the type of processes used to dispense, package, and ship the particular concentrate product. These are called our *levers*.
2.　　　The second level of detail is in focusing on zooming into the smallest interval of change that the business operationally deals with, in order to identify the quasi-linear effect in that space.

To illustrate the first level of analysis, let us perform a quick *bounded analysis of theoretical water inputs* as an example model. Over the lifetime of a plant, you could theoretically say that a plant could consume anywhere between zero and a million gallons of water. However, we know that not to be practically true. A plant that consumes zero water will die very quickly, and a plant that tries to consume a million gallons of water will drown. And trying to model a plant's consumption of water from the interval of zero gallons and a million gallons can be a very non-linear model. It could be exponential; it could be sinusoidal (there could be a very large dip). And it would be very hard to model mathematically.

However, what I have discovered in my research, and what the theory of *strategic bounded analysis (SPA)* provides, is that if you are able to identify the boundaries through which a product or a lever most typically operates, what happens is, by looking within those boundaries of that space, you are able to actually better understand and have control over the outputs, and a better understanding of what might actually be going on. It's like zooming into the part of the model that most reflects the business objectives. So, instead of thinking of a plant taking anywhere between zero and a million gallons of water, which could very clearly be a non-linear model, if you basically bound your decision-making scope to the typical interval for the amount of water that's consumed, let's say between 100 and 200 gallons over the lifetime of that plant, then what you'll notice is that, in most of these cases, the model in that bounded interval is almost linear. Even if you're not a data scientist, this is much easier to understand and a much easier model from which to produce actionable results and develop strategies.

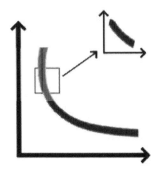

Illustration of Bounded Analysis.

The ultimate idea is that by performing a bounded analysis, managers and data scientists can meet in the middle and be able to communicate and understand what certain levers exist and what type of changes might need to be made along the interval to help affect the ultimate consumer's experience and drive revenue, profits, and growth for the company.

Parts 3 and 4 of this book uses bounded analysis as its primary way of illustrating the data science and the numbers that drive each aspect of the data pipeline.

The other important factor in providing a common language for data science and for regulation as the industry is growing, is that there are many different players coming in, either organically or from other industries. Cannabis is a crop. And just like any crop, there's been hundreds of years of institutional knowledge with regards to agriculture. So you have people who are organically growing their companies through the cannabis industry, or they're transferring knowledge from other industries to get a foothold with their *institutional knowledge advantage.*

Dissecting Convolutional Markets (CMs)

Another important consideration in establishing a common

reference language is that it creates a scientific guide to the units and standardization of the existing industry technologies and ways of measuring progress and units within the different processes that govern the consumer experience. You should look more closely at this introduction to convolutional markets as economic phenomena that are driving the future of all commerce. Everyone within an organization, from CEOs to the point of sales clerk, are already being affected by *convolutional markets*, or *CMs*, as I'll interchangeably refer to them. The idea of CMs is meant to prepare you and your business to adapt and capitalize.

CMs are a recent economic phenomenon because of the decreasing cost of manufacturing technology, combined with a growing prevalence of big data in consumer product optimization. CMs use data to collect information about not just the manufacturing process, but the consumer's reaction toward the result of the manufacturing process. This data then feeds back into the manufacturing system, from tuning the speed of the conveyor belt to adding a bit of taste adjustment for the consumers. The rise of CMs are a product of two important developments in recent history:

1. the need for markets to always specialize to satisfy consumer tastes, or, as we say, hyper-personalization; and
2. the rise of data science as a driving force in industrial strategy.

The core of the book's research on CMs is centered on the cannabis market in Part 3 and 4, but we spend the remainder of Part 2 introducing CMs through several different other market examples.

Convolutional markets are markets with memory, as we've pointed out.

Simply put, a CM is a scalable market where a consumer's tastes are uniquely, fully, and systematically satisfied and internalized within that market, affecting the structure of the market itself. Unlike normal competitive markets, CMs by their nature converge toward a state where they're able to provide every single consumer within that market a unique experience, tailored directly to them, or hyper-personalized to them (Baron, 2019).

In contrast, a default market, or *DM*, in the traditional economic sense, provides a place of transaction for the average taste of the *normal distribution* of consumers in the proximity of that market, responding to the rules of supply and demand to find a price equilibrium. A CM, however, provides a place of transaction for the specific taste of the *uniform distribution* of consumer in the proximity of that market, responding with a constant price. This means the market responds to the preferences of the consumer by acknowledging that a consumer's preferences "belongs to every single person and is unique to every single person" (Combinator, 2018).

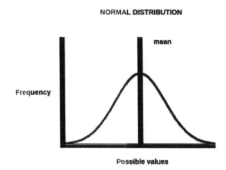

Illustration of Normal Distribution.

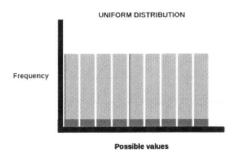

Illustration Uniform Distribution.

This is a critical distinction, because a market with actual memory is a market that will put equal weight on all data that comes into that market, hence the uniform distribution. When a market does not remember the data well, then it has to discount old data versus new data, giving an exponential distribution with decay. In a similar case, if you're looking over averages and you are assuming a normal distribution, that will also adjust your perspective. The reality is, if you're able to take data and crystallize it in a standardized and regularized form (and responsively store it), then there's no reason that the data that is five to 10 years old should be less weighted than data that is currently being collected, unless of course data points, i.e. consumers, have fallen out of your market.

CMs follow directly the path and the idea that data is highly monetizable and very valuable to companies. In fact, many companies, including Google and Facebook, do a lot of work just to collect your data. The ability to monetize and then create actionable insight from this data is part of the idea in the growing convolutional markets and understanding of markets with memory. You want to understand an idea and gain the ability to not only create strategy at the managerial level but to introduce tactics of analysis at the data science level that work together to further your company's goals and grow.

Within a CM, How Do You Measure Consumer Satisfaction?

Within a CM, how do you determine if the person is completely satisfied? Well, if an infinite amount of money wouldn't improve their satisfaction, and you have evaluated their needs and could not find another basket of goods that could make them happier, then the person is completely satisfied. The other interesting property about the convolutional market is that there is no *moral hazard problem* when it comes to human recommenders. Since the consumer is directly providing feedback about the product, and there is no incentive by any other party to alter that taste profile in order to manipulate the consumer, and they are responding directly to the market, then it is possible to maximize market efficiency, because the market will be responding directly back to the consumer.

Before the advent of data science and real-time data feedback technologies, the *convolutional time* of a product potentially resulting in any improvements, flavor enhancement, or innovation (i.e. the *innovation cycle*), would have been the entire life-cycle of the product.

This is the first time in human history that the convolution time of a product is less than one lifecycle, and decreasing do to technological advances. Or rather, stated differently, that the change in the supply chain to match consumer flavor and information feedback can be instantaneous.

How does this instantaneous feedback mathematically model? In economics, we say that the market fully endogenizes the utility profile of the consumer. Starting with price and quantity, the flavor is a distribution of fully consumed quantity, where there is no data loss in the measurement of input COGS (Cost of Goods Sold). So, then once the flavor profile is fully modeled and endogenized, you have the function that is then a price and quantity as a function of flavor and COGS. Whereas flavor was not an input into the function originally.

So the question is: what would happen to a market (the quantity and price of products), if the flavor profile of each consumer could be internalized along the entire value chain of the market, using technology, data science, and economic theory? Ultimately, we'll look at this bounded analysis, end points, the different data channels along the pipeline, and the resulting outcome is a commoditized and fully convolutional market that touches every part of the supply chain, from seed to sale to consumer.

A fully convoluted network or market doesn't distinguish between the population flavor and a frictionless action towards local flavor preferences. Either way, that's how things converge, or tip, depending on the barrier in place. There are other foundational parts of economics that also help support this. In information asymmetry or game theory, it is either one-way or two-way process, not a multi-dimensional process that acts as a feedback system. In behavioral economics, the focus is primarily on prospect theory, game theory, and information asymmetry. There's also mechanism design theory, which involves similar feedback loops, but does not involve the memory component - the market remembers. Ultimately we can think of the market for consumer preferences as series of auctions where producers are bidding with their products to satisfy said preferences. Using the concept of revenue equivalence, we know that the structure of the auction does not matter, and that net resulting outcomes will be the same. That is because humans naturally adjust their estimates via market signals, as was pointed out by Nobel Laureate in Economics William Vickrey (Arrow et al., 1997).

But what if the flavor preferences within a market are a finite resource, like crude oil? Once oil was reduced into commodity products and all its flavors were commoditized, it had been completely convoluted, like art, which is all entirely based on an auction. In the end, the only elements that can be improved in this process are the mechanisms for optimization, which can be mechanical, technological, or physical capital related, and/or the human capital involved in the improvement mechanism. Convolutional markets will eventually capture all of the consumer preferences. Like a high-end makeup or perfume brand, every smell and color shade against every skin type is just about mapped to nearly a bijection function (Thein and Lin, 2003).

So, what are the markets that are going to end up in convolutional convergence? The market where the product is one of three things:

1.   A reproducible product, which can be made on an assembly line (like a plant field - not like an original painting). The market has infinite product capability and reproducibility;
2.   The product inputs and outputs are a closed form system, where every input can be measured and identified;
3.   And lastly, the nature of the convolution convergence is based on a perfectly assembled vertical stack of data, collecting a complete population data set through a pipeline that captures the population data set, and not just samples.

The CM Spectrum: Where does the Contemporary Cannabis Market Stand? (Part 3 of 5)

A convolutional market can be seen as being in one of five degrees along a spectrum, the middle stage of which explains what the cannabis industry is currently experiencing. For example, in cannabis today, if you want to create the "perfect experience" for a particular consumer, there are two ways of effectively doing so.

On one hand, a consumer could hire a team of PhD scientists and spend anywhere between one and 10 million dollars building an entire facility, taking genetic engineering of the plant, as well as genetic data from the consumer, growing a perfect singular plant, harvesting it, cutting it, and then rolling it into what might be a joint.

On the other hand, a consumer could fill out a questionnaire, their biometric data could be read (at a very inexpensive existing technological cost), and that information could be put into a magical synthesizing machine. This machine then uses a machine learning model to identify the exact *terpene and cannabinoid* profile that is required to accommodate the taste and needs of that consumer. This synthesizer will then inject the chemical synthetically into a leaf, which then could be rolled into a joint.

Now, if you put both of these joints in front of a person, and they were to consume both of them, from the perspective of the consumer, their *utility* (or amount of positive consumer experience) would be exactly the same. However, in one case, it costs over a million dollars to develop this perfect plant made for a single person, while in the other case, the technology to synthesize the experience might have cost pennies on the dollar. But from the perspective and the utility of the consumer, the product is exactly the same. Thus, whether you've spent a million dollars on the strain or 10 dollars on the strain, from the perspective of the utility of the consumer, there is no difference.

That is the nature of convolutional markets. As a market diverges from its middle ground, there's a tipping point where a market can go either left or right in the graph, but in the end, it will actually settle. As the market diverges and there's two different types of ways of providing an experience for the consumer, in the end, through the enabling of big data, you're able to virtualize that experience in a hyper-personalized way, such that once the market becomes fully commoditized, which usually ends up in an aesthetic way diverging into what is called the barbell distribution within an industry, where you have super high-end boutiques and you have then lower and cheaper consumables. But from the perspective of the consumer, they're exactly the same experience or same satisfaction utility. An example of a market that can also diverge into a barbell is the modern beer market in America. The market sustains both large, mass-production brands, as well as crafter brewers for those individuals with niche tastes (Stangler & Litan, 2009).

Sub-CM: Household Climate Control (Part 1 of 5)

What are other examples of markets that also follow this trend? We'll start at the very left side of the graph, the extreme, using the example of super personalized-technologies (like air, heat, and cooling systems for residential homes). On the right of this graph, you have a very low cost of technology, where sensors that measure temperature and humidity (elements that might affect the comfort of a person in a house) can cost cents on the dollar. Because of the decreasing cost of technology, you can place these sensors everywhere and continuously collect data inexpensively. In this case, the data pipeline, as well as the technology, has been largely commoditized. We're able to collect a very large amount of data, inexpensively, because of the rapid decreasing cost of technology that drives the collection of this data and the feedback of the system.

For example on the right side of the spectrum, we see the Nest system for keeping a household at the perfect temperature for its resident. A Nest system collects consumer data, then sends it into the cloud, where algorithms are performed on the instantaneously to adjust temperatures. In this case, the temperature regulation (since it is effectively costless to run the algorithm in the cloud and collect that data) feeds data back to your HVAC system to adjust the temperature at low cost. The minimized and commoditized cost of technology to execute this system has enabled, on the right side of the convolutional market curve, to have a completely personalized experience for the consumer (Yang and Newman, 2013).

Why is the decreasing cost of technology due to commoditization important? Let's consider the amount it costs to use a reading light, for example. At one time, a reading light by candle would have required several hours of human work. Today, the cost to have several hours of reading light is low, given the invention of the light bulb. This is due to commoditization, through decreasing technological costs of a particular human experience. The consumer is indifferent as to where their light is coming from, as long as it is sufficient for reading -- in which case they will take the option that involves the least investment of their resources. Ultimately, utility is about the fringes of the human experience, as it is observed by the consumer. Markets are driven by maximizing that. Industries and companies gain a majority market share by fine tuning their services to capture the taste and preference of the consumer.

Sub-CM: Alternative Energy (Part 2 of 5)

Now, what is the next industry on the spectrum to the left? It is an industry that is slightly less commoditized, but also has a similar experience. Instead of a market for personal consumption of a particular climate-controlled experience, as we might call it, the next most similar system (but where the medium of that technology has not been fully commoditized and is not yet at its minimum) would be renewable energy options, where people gain satisfaction and their utility by purchasing electricity from a source that they know might be renewable. This might give them a positive benefit and good feeling, because

49

they know that they're potentially doing something to help the planet. Most Corporate Social Responsibility (CSR) missions fall in this category.

How does this look in terms of a convolutional market? Well, it's basically the same as the farthest right and the Nest sensing technology, except that the technology itself has not been fully commoditized, thus it's not at a price minimum. When you're purchasing renewable energy options, you're willing to pay slightly more for an energy source that isn't a core fossil fuel, which is fully commoditized, or usually at a price minimum. Then there's a flavor feedback system that is also nearly commoditized. The flavor internalization is also nearly commoditized, because companies are so in tune with the flavor, they even know how to make tax breaks for you in order to make your choices more attractive (Painuly, 2001). They know that you can acquire tax breaks to adopt the technology, or potentially acquire renewable energy (Burns & Kang, 2012).

Understanding this, you see that as you're going to the right of the spectrum, for the *medium of manufacture* (the medium through which the product is delivered to the consumer), the trend is to the right, the medium of manufacture or the *flavor internalization system* (how you ask consumers about their feedback and how you respond to it) either totally diverges toward the public domain and biological fundamentals, or toward externalized expertise where the flavor is fully exogenized. Either way you have a function that can explain it by either one single point source person, or the entire population dataset. The important thing about a fully convolutional market is that a single point source person is equivalently observable as an entire population data set because the utilities are the same.

Sub-CM: Luxury Perfume: A left side example (Part 4 of 5)

Now getting back to the cannabis market, we can see that nothing is fully commoditized in this space. Although it is not fully commoditized, we see that the cost of technology trend slowly decreasing -- currently the cost of equipment is decreasing (although slowly - which is preventing entrance to market for some players) and we are able to process more volumes of cannabis and its derivatives through these advancements in technology and speed. So, let's say the left side of the spectrum of cannabis that we have increasing specificity and flavors. We look at the perfume and makeup fashion market where the medium of the market in precision products is very commoditized. The technology is expensive because extracting and making long lasting colognes requires a lot of science and research and has to be individually tailored. The flavor feedback system is highly commoditized, meaning that the choice of smells is reserved to executive artists and tastemakers. This creates a human capital element where the flavor feedback system is highly commoditized, but then you have flavor internalization, which is full transparency in the background. This means that flavor internalization has been fully commoditized and perfumes that sell will ultimately stay in a market that is natural and stated in economic theory.

Sub-CM: High-end Art: A left side example (Part 5 of 5)

On the far left side of the CM spectrum are the ultimate luxury markets, like the high-end art market. In the context of a high-end art market, as a medium, the medium is commoditized, but the product is completely unreproducible, unlike the scale where the technology is infinitely commoditized and cheap.

Nima Veiseh

The canvas paint is worthless by itself, however, the medium is fully commoditized in the high-end art market. There are many agents but only one option. Thus, people have infinite access but must adhere to a price given by a single availability. When you buy a single piece of original art, it cannot be reproduced.

However, we must note that a $100M Picasso painting may not give you 100M times more satisfaction than a $1 donut. That is because of the prospect theory concept of diminishing sensitivity tells us that our enjoyment with respect to an input does not grow linearly, and in fact dissipates (Tversky et al., 1991).

Now, on the flip side, the example of the art market convolving completely is in its ability to create realistic prints and reproduce them at very low cost. For example, every man, woman, and child can have a Mona Lisa in their private room because commoditized printing technology has reduced that cost so much. Also similar in the high end art market, and what makes this interesting as a case, is that the flavor feedback system has also been commoditized into a liquid auction market, say at Christie's or Sotheby's. However, instead of diverging to accommodate the flavor of anyone who enters the room as might be the case in a nest system as described on the right side of the spectrum, instead it converges to one single person with a specialized skill. That painter is the one who created the painting and nothing else can replace that human capital element.

The important thing to note is that the data pipeline we're going to discuss has elements of both sides of the convolutional market, both with strictly irreplaceable human capital element, like a grower with specialized skills. And at the same time, a highly commoditized sensing technology infrastructure, which is thousands of combined sensors in a Nest System that help to collect data and provide feedback on the process. These two pieces work together along each stage of the pipeline.

On the right side of the spectrum, we talk about flavor internalization with respect to art. We say the flavor internalization is fully commoditized and that you have countless art publications and full transparency of ownership history, which is actually the market with memory. In art, whoever owned the art piece and the memory of the art piece can affect the price just as much as the quality of the impact the art makes on a consumer who has no idea about the history.

Conversely, on the far right side of the graph there is also full transparency on the ownership history as well. Technologies like Blockchain also help with this, as discussed later in the book. All the ownership data has been fully consumed and internalized by the system. But in the end, whether you approach the left side or the right side of the graph, the graph then turns back on itself to converge to a point where the utility is the same. No matter how much you spend, if you either go very cheap or very expensive across the whole system, and how much you invest in the infrastructure, you will still get the same satisfaction from the perspective of the consumer.

A fully convoluted market does not distinguish the population flavor and a frictionless access toward measuring agent level flavors. Either way, that's how things converge or tip depending on the barriers in place at inception. Kylie Jenner is a perfect example of someone that crossed both directions by simultaneously focusing the flavor feedback system to diverging toward her unique ability to design, while at the same time distributing the intelligence via all of Instagram making a flat market with little barrier-to-entry. In the end, the result is the same. You have one super taster or one human capital person that can't be replaced. Similar to the idea, although algorithms will govern our behavior, a human still has to write the algorithms (Harari, 2016). Someone who has the intelligence to program the algorithm and add real value. All convolutional markets will ultimately monetize and surrender their memory to the supply chain and the only person left will be the one modeling the algorithm, and that is ultimately purely intangible and dependent on the human operator that is helping to guide the market.

Currently, in any convolutional market, the human element and the human capital element cannot be removed. It can only be reduced to the accountability of one decision maker or one programmer or one executive making those decisions. This is the full spectrum of convolutional markets and in the future it is critical for executives, managers, and data scientists alike to understand the full pipeline of a data system, because systems engineering is ultimately how you make something to create value that is greater than the sum of its parts.

Macro Convolutional Markets

This last section touches on convolutional markets but at the macro level. Instead of looking at the consumer in a specific private market, we will consider what convolutional markets can tell us in the transformation of governments and institutions from the perspective of their consumer, the citizen. So if convolutional markets are about systems that serve the citizen, where can we see potential breakdowns in convolutional markets as they start to now serve their consumers. First and foremost, convolutional markets are where observational truth, in the form of data, is processed and distributed in such a way that all players in the market can help to better serve the consumer. In other words, people are accountable in the system through merit, which allows them to collect and act on the data they receive. If they respond to the data in a way that benefits the consumer, that speaks positively to their merit as an agent of the convolutional market, and vice versa. Whenever accountability is allocated by anything except merit, it seems to polarize into one of two forms-- extreme communism, or extreme socialism. In either form, especially at a governance level, this polarization seems to lead to instability. In either case, the instability is a result of the data and observational truths not properly reaching decision makers who would act on behalf of the constituents; instead, the decision makers are internalizing their own self interest.

Thesis: all markets are turning into convolutional markets, including at the macroeconomic scale. This is why Twitter and big data now seem to affect elections in ways that are unanticipated and quicker than ever before.

One example of this polarization is the experiment of communism in Russia, which ended with the dissolution of the Soviet Union in 1991. In Part 1, we touched on the relationship between the Chernobyl disaster and the collapse of the Soviet Union. It might seem that giving everyone the same position and power might lead to a flat means of communication. However, what ended up actually being the case is that information did not move from those with the facts -- the scientists -- to the decision makers. In communism, human capital is effectively commoditized, meaning no functioning labor market, and their input does not factor into any impact for the system. Commoditizing those who are trying to speak up, whether a scientist or a citizen, is effectively removing the empowerment of those at the bottom who were accountable but they actually were given no voice. Any power dynamic, no matter how flat and intentioned to serve the people, will collapse under the weight of a lack of accountability. By giving everyone the same position and preventing data from directionally flowing from those with the ability to report to those with the ability to act, accountability is difficult to resolve.

The end of the Cold War seems to have marked an end to the question of communism, however, has the same consideration been made of capitalism? Is capitalism the answer or could it face a similar issue?

Currently, what we appear to be seeing in the United States is a similar lack of accountability. Voice within governance is being given disproportionately to some through the redistribution of wealth. That redistribution of wealth is not being directly mandated through competitive markets, but are rather functions of intervening institutions that are disconnected from explicit merit. Examples of this include lobbied reductions in wealth taxes, private campaign financing and tax breaks to corporate "productive" interests where there is no agent or atomicity in accountability. By giving a disproportionate voice to some, the observational truths don't get heard by those with the power to affect decisions, and it hurts accountability. Accountability only has value if it has a voice. The improperly distributed voice is correlated with growing inequality in the wealth distribution.

So why not have a revolution? Because going from one extreme to another does not seem to be that helpful. In a capitalist revolution, the accountability is placed exclusively on the consumer, forcing accountability up the hierarchy, and placing the burden of incremental decision progress on the managers. On the other extreme, a communist revolution takes accountability and places it exclusively in the hands of the command economy decision maker, and forcing accountability down, placing the incremental decision process on the individual citizens.

While both of these extremes are only theoretical, they illustrate an important dichotomy in terms of the need for institutions, accountability and regulation. In the communist example, the economy is under-regulated from the perspective of the consumer, often resulting in bad quality goods produced. In the capitalism extreme, the economy is under-regulated from the perspective of the decision maker, which leads to bad business practices favoring managers.

Russia is an interesting case study of having done both, working under a communist system and a capitalist system. In both cases, it finds economic instability and without intermediate institutions to manage the economy. Ultimately, it doesn't matter what system of government you are under, if the rules governing accountability are no longer in play.

What is in the Remainder of this Book in Parts 3 and 4?

We will explore the industry in sections. From the beginning, profits, seed-to-sale and all the way through to definitions and a number of metrics.

As an industry first, this book also contains a statistical analysis of different parts of the supply chain. In 2018 and 2019 during my work as an academic researcher, as well as working within a data incubator, I was able to create the first ever taste analysis in the industry, based off of public and semi-private data sets. I began with the core question: what are the factors and levers that actually impact the consumer experience? This analysis will help to shape the foundation of what is considered to be "cutting edge" and gives us an opportunity to optimize within the industry. We expect that in the years to come, this analysis will be updated, and we'll see from the perspective of the economic historian, what type of changes are being made and how this analysis will be enriched as this market convolves. Future editions of this book will highlight these changes.

This book is meant to serve as a guide and basis of understanding for effective communication within the industry. It will provide a foundational framework for the industry that lasts through the coming years.

Let's dive in.

PART 3: GROWTH AND PREDICTING THE PRESENT: WHAT DOES DATA SCIENCE NEED TO KNOW ABOUT MANAGING THE CANNABIS ECONOMY?

"Every input that can be measured that ultimately affects the consumer is a data point that the data science team needs to know about managing the cannabis economy."

This section of the book reviews the entire data pipeline of the cannabis industry process. Whether you are a data scientist or business leader, it is important to understand how each input factors into your final product and the resulting experience for the consumer. The goal for any company trying to affect their convolutional market and maximize consumer satisfaction should be to understand, document and measure every part of their data pipeline along their supply chain. This is what we mean by a *vertically integrated data pipeline*. Every input that can be measured that ultimately affects the consumer is a data point that the data science team needs to know about managing the cannabis economy. Before we can be *prescriptive* with our data analysis, we must be *descriptive*.

Every section of Part 3 will quantify a part of the industry supply chain and provide a scientific explanation for the background and measurements available for each part of the data pipeline.

Overview of Seed to Sale Flow Diagram.

Before we dive in, a few important pieces of information:

To give you a very quick overview, the first section and con-
tinuation of this book, as it relates to the industry, is the micro
data pipeline (which is the data science in the cannabis market).
What does it look like? How does seed-to-sale in the feedback
loop get structured? How does the government promote data
keeping? What are the policy-related issues with changes at the
state and federal level? What are the data silos and how do we
merge them? What are issues of data security and data mining?
How does data affect machine learning in the cloud?

Looking at macro data (finance) and observing the industry at
a macro level, we can consider: additional macro inputs (which
includes the public policy perspective, international legal,
and different federal implications); legal differences between
American states and the federal regulations; as well as taxation
within the United States and Canada:

- seeds, genetics and the misunderstanding between
plant types;
- infrastructure and plotting in relation to how you grow
things;
- cultivation, initial growth stages, and the chemistry
of the plant;
- harvesting, drying and pruning the plant;
- packaging and preserving the plants;
- humidity control and types of packaging (the future of
packaging)
- shipping and transporting cannabis products across
state lines;
- dispensaries, retail cannabis consumption, delivery
mechanisms;
- feedback from the recreational consumer, feedback
from the medicinal consumer:

- CBD versus THC.

The Seed to Soil

"The plant's genome and genetic history certainly does have an effect on the consumer experience, affecting everything from terpene profile to crop yields."

History of the Plant, Genetic Origins and Basic Characteristics

The first stage of the data pipeline starts with the seed. The seed can be measured many different ways; for example, the mass and the color of the seed can both be observed, measured, and recorded. The mass and color of the seed, however, are examples of two measures that we will not include in the data pipeline. Why? Because they are not known in any way to affect the outcome of the plant, thus affecting the experience of the consumer. Think of it this way—the color and size of the shipping truck your Amazon packages arrive in do not normally factor into your consumer experience with the actual product.

A measurement of the seed that has become increasingly discussed in recent years, however, is the genetic makeup of the seed. This is also known as its *genetic sequence*, or *genome*. The plant's genome and genetic history certainly does have an effect on the consumer experience, affecting everything from terpene profile to crop yields. It is best that we introduce these factors upfront to have an understanding about what type of levers factor into the utility of the consumer and their overall satisfaction. This plant is a living thing that's been documented through big data and will evolve through a convolutional market, but to understand how it characterizes in different ways, we're going to talk about the history and genetics of this plant. A deep dive into the science of genetics is beyond the scope of this book, so instead we will be providing an overview of the evolutionary path of the plan and a genetic history that form the foundations of the plant.

Traditionally, cannabis is known in two different varieties, either *sativa* or *indica*, but the truth is that cannabis is actually derived from a single ancestral species. The tea plant from which the hot beverage is brewed, is similar in that most varieties of tea are actually from the genetic same plant. Regardless of whether sativas or indicas are genetically different from each other, indica is considered a putative species of the genus Cannabis. So, Cannabis indica is actually scientifically known as Cannabis sativa in the form of indica (Gleichmann, 2019).

Cannabis indica and *Cannabis sativa* do have visual differences. For example, *Cannabis sativa* is characterized by being a taller plant, typically between six and 12 feet, with internodal spacing. It also tends to have longer growth cycles. Indica plants however tend to be shorter, have smaller *internodal distances* and *shorter cycles*, resulting in different ratios of the two known psychoactive components, tetrahydrocannabinol (THC) and cannabidiol (CBD). We'll be going into these momentarily in greater detail.

Cannabis indica is traditionally thought to have come from the areas of Afghanistan and northern Pakistan where you find their namesakes, or *land race strains* (like Afghan Kush and Hindu Kush) to be prevalent, whereas sativa plants originated in warmer equatorial climates that have longer growing seasons. Hence the longer time to maturity and higher THC contents. THC is tetrahydrocannabinol, a crystalline compound that is the main active ingredient of cannabis. CBD is short for cannabidiol, a molecule found in the cannabis plant (Atakan, 2012).

There is another genetically distinct plant and species, *Cannabis ruderalis*, first described by Russian botanist, D.E. Janischewsky in 1924 (Janischewsky, 1924). The Ruderalis is an important component in the ecosystem of cannabis because it is able to auto flower. This means that this plant *Cannabis ruderalis* transitions from a vegetative state to a flowering stage with age, as opposed to the light cycle required with photoperiod strains like *Cannabis indica* and *Cannabis sativa*.

Similarly, auto flowering plants like *C. ruderalis* have higher CBD content and they tend to flower earlier in the life cycle than the photoperiod cannabis plant. The Ruderalis plant can be crossbred with indicas and sativas to have a potency of THC comparable to sativas and indicas while also providing auto flowering capabilities of the seeds. This auto flowering is called an *auto flowering phenotype*. *Cannabis ruderalis* is often found in areas where hemp cultivation was once prevalent, including in the midwestern United States and in places like Eastern Europe with a more rigorous climate.

Cannabis indica was discovered much earlier by Jean-Baptiste Lamarck in 1785. *Cannabis sativa* was formally classified by Carl Linnaeus in 1753. Unlike *Cannabis ruderalis*, which is auto-flowering, the *C. sativa* and *C. indica* are light-dependent. Female sativa and indica plants produce seeds only when pollinated by male plants; however, cultivators typically prevent plants from producing seeds because that drains energy and resources away from the plant that could be going into THC cultivation, where the economic value of an indica or sativa cannabis plant is derived. Feminized seeds are popular among commercial seed suppliers create artificially hermaphroditic females. Seed production can also be induced or prevented by treating the plants with hormones or a compound known as *silver thiosulfate*.

There are many chemicals that go into these plants, that are related to these plants that we'll discuss as inputs that go into the work of a plant. We'll review, but primarily it's water management that affects growth characteristics. Just like any plant, nutrients, water, light and circulated air at a maintained temperature can be optimized to maximize the output of the plant. As far as internal chemicals that matter to the consumer? There are more than 500 compounds within the plant in addition to THC and CBD. The final product quality and quantity reflect an interaction between the genetics of the pants and the conditions maintained for its growth.

The Start of the Data Pipeline: Seed Tagging

To maintain the integrity of the data pipeline and confidence in the data that is being received, it is important to know exactly every hand that interacts with the seed and process from start to finish. That is why policy makers are encouraging efforts in the industry for seed tagging. Seed tagging is a way of marking a seed before it is ever cultivated into a plant, and allows us to know. This has positive ramifications for policy makers, because it allows accountability for the output of the plant, to be tracked from the very beginning of the process. That also means that any adverse effects that may ever occur due to the consumption of a particular seed can be easily tracked to the source and remedied. Seed tagging involves registering the genetic identifiers of a seed that can point to the exact wholesaler, and even the crop that the plant was harvested from. The data pipeline starts with seed tagging.

Genetic Varieties, Landrace Strains and Heirloom Strains

All plants and animals genetically come from somewhere. All 2,832 genetically distinct strains registered to the Leafly database at the time of publication of this book are derived from genetically isolated pure strains characterized and cultivated for their unique attributes (Leafly, 2019). These are known as *landrace* strains (Hillig, 2005). These strains are also unique in the sense that they have been domesticated and locally adapted to different parts of the world.

Landrace strains: the parent strains and the most genetically pure strains, from which all other strains are derived (Hillig, 2003).

The direct descendants from landrace strains are called *heirloom strains*. Then from there we have our nearly 3,000 currently *hybridized and crossbred cannabis strains* (de Meijer & Van Soest, 1992). Hybrid strains may be hardier and more adaptable, but will produce less consistent product until a seed stock is established. Depending on the type of environment in which it lives, a plant that's more likely to manifest as a sativa or indica is likely to survive due to the physical characteristics that allow it to grow and adapt to that specific region of the world. Typically when someone commercially consumes a strain, it's not an original landrace or heirloom strain but rather one of the hybridized strains (Small, 2015).

Of the landrace strains, the shorter, stockier, sturdier plants tend to be the indicas -- the Kushes and the Afghans. (Hindu Kush and Afghani are two Indicas that originated around the Kush mountain range of the Afghanistan-Pakistan border and the Afghan greater area respectively). As far as the Sativa strains, we'll notice that they tend to propagate and thrive in warmer climates, known by names like Thailand, Panama Red from Panama, Durban Poison from the Durban area of South Africa, Punto Rojo from Columbia, Acapulco Gold from Mexico, Lambsbread from Jamaica, Malawi from Malawi Africa and Luang Prabang from Laos. From these landrace strains all other strains are derived genetically.

What is the Difference between Hemp and Cannabis?

Hemp and Cannabis plants have similar appearances, but a closer look at each plant offers up very clear distinctions. Cannabis features broad leaves, dense buds, and a stocky, bushy appearance. In contrast, hemp features skinny leaves that are concentrated toward the top of the plant. When put side by side, the two plants are easy to distinguish. Hemp and cannabis also possess crucial differences in their chemical composition and the types of cannabinoids they produce. Hemp has a very low concentration of THC (0.3% or less) (Bosca et al., 1997). Cannabis is abundant in THC with concentrations between 15 and 40 percent (Mehmedic et al., 2010). Because of this distinction, hemp is grown for industrial purposes, while cannabis is grown for recreational or medicinal purposes.

To give more historical context, hemp likely originated in Central Asia. The cultivation of this plant for fiber was recorded in China as early as 2800 BCE and was practiced in Europe, as well, early on, spreading throughout the entirety of Europe during the Middle Ages (Li & Lin, 1974). Hemp made its way to South America in the 1500s and a century later to North America.(Zuardi, 2006). Over time, the use of industrial hemp has evolved into an even greater variety of products, including health foods, organic body care, clothing, construction materials, biofuels, plastic composites and more (according to one source, more than 25,000 products can be made from hemp) (Ranalli and Venturi, 2004).

According to the U.S. Department of Agriculture, the agency that regulates hemp production, industrial hemp includes the plant *Cannabis sativa* and any part or derivative of such plant (including the seeds) whether growing or not, that is used exclusively for industrial purposes, fiber and flower with a tetrahydrocannabinol concentration of not more than 0.3% on a dry weight basis (USDA, 2018).

CBD and THC

Among the roughly 500 compounds known to be part of the cannabis plant, over 120 are *cannabinoids* (like THC and CBD), which bond to certain receptors within the body in order to create an experience for the consumer (Munro et al., 1993). The chemical composition of these compounds can be defined in three families. Aside from *cannabinoids*, which may or may not have a psychoactive effect and bind to certain receptors, there are also *terpenes*, which are chemicals that give the aroma and effect of the plant as it is consumed (Singh & Sharma, 2015). These terpenes I have found through my economic analysis are just as important to the experience of a consumer as is the brand of the strain or the psychoactive THC or CBD levels. The third category are known as flavonoids, which are other plant chemical byproducts that can affect everything from the plants color to the observed taste of the plant when consumed. There are over 6,000 known flavonoids in the plant kingdom (Panche et al., 2016).

The *Endocannabinoid system*, or ECS, is a network of system of molecular signals (called neurotransmitters) and receptors in our bodies. The cannabis plant contains molecules that can act as external inputs to these receptors (Console-Bram et al. 2012). The two main receptors for cannabinoids are CB1 receptors and CB2 receptors. CB1 receptors target motor activity, thinking, motor coordination, appetite, short term memory, pain perception and immune cells (Calignano et al., 1998). The CB2 receptors are much broader than CB1 and influence most of the body, which can include gut, kidneys, pancreas, skeletal muscle, bone, eye, reproductive system, immune system, respiratory tract, skin, the cardiovascular system and liver.

As noted, the sensors are found in different specific and select tissues. In addition to the cannabinoids, there are terpenes. The added effects terpenes have on a consumer's experience is what we call the *entourage effect* (Ben-Shabat et al., 1998). For the recreational consumer, the total experience is a natural combination of the psychoactive cannabinoid components, non-psychoactive cannabinoids, and the terpenes all being absorbed and processed by the body, similar to how smell can affect the taste of a food and how certain senses have different dependencies. The entourage effect helps us to better understand how terpenes, despite not having an actual psychoactive effect, can enhance the perception and experience of the consumer through the cannabinoids and psychoactive compounds (Williamson & Evans, 2000).

Consider the following profiles of different cannabinoids:

-THC-A or tetrahydrocannabinolic acid is the most common cannabinoid. It's found in both the sativa or indica cannabis plants, and is a non-psychoactive and is a precursor of THC. THC-A converts to THC through an organic chemical reaction of hydrolysis where the reaction of THC-A releases THC.

-THC or tetrahydrocannabinol, is the primary psychoactive substance in the sativa and indica plants. THC is decarboxylated typically with the help of heat and has been changed from THC-A. It is also the most well known of all cannabinoids.

-CBD-A or cannabidiolic acid, is one of four different compounds that emerged from CBG-A. When CBD-A is decarboxylated, it typically becomes CBD.

-CBD or Cannabidiol, is the principal non-psychoactive cannabinoid in the sativa and indica plants. Although it is not psychoactive, it has a range of physical and psychological effects.

-CBN or Cannabinol, is THC that is exposed to oxygen and heat (has experienced a redox reaction) and will eventually convert into CBN. CBN is mildly psychoactive and still has many therapeutic effects that are still being researched.

-CBG or cannabigerol, is considered the mother cannabinoid. CBG can be metabolized into different cannabinoids and drastically change the plant. Just like we discussed before, CBD-A is one of four results of CBG-A. CBG by itself is not psychoactive acting as a contrast to THC. CBG can have effects that are anti-bacterial, anti-tumorigenic, and can promote neurogenesis.

Measuring Seeds and Seed Production Characteristics

Rating seeds in the seed industry occurs via several metrics that indicate the type of work and metrics involved. Let me provide an overview of these different metrics (Rahn et al., 2016).

Binary Variable Metric

The first metric dictates whether the plant or the seed is auto-flowering or not. This is the *binary variable*. It is presented as a true/false indicator (Manski, 1987). In computer science, we also refer to binary variables as *booleans*.

Available auto-flowering seeds are White Dwarf, Red Dwarf, Syrup, Magnum, Budda Pink Kush as well as Vesta and Calamity Jane. Some that are not are Quasar, Kraken and Pulsar (Potter, 2014).

Seeds in a pre-federal legalization era are typically sold as either *regular* or *auto-flowering* (meaning they are either sold as feminized or regular seeds). There's another binary variable present dictating whether it is *feminized* or a *regular* seed.

Indoors vs. Outdoors

An important binary variable involved with seeds is whether you want to cultivate flower *indoors* or *outdoors*. This will impact the equipment, flowering timeline, and overall approach that a grower will take to optimize growth throughout the plant's life-cycle.

Number of Genetic Generations Metric

Another metric of the flower that's important to note is the *number of genetic generations* that the strain is backed by. This number can be as low as single digits. The seed can have as little as zero generations or even more than 40, with the common numbers between 5 and 15 generations helping to create adapted generations of plants that have selected the best traits, made for each of the parents, for more than 50 generations. It enables the growers to emphasize production, speed and aromatic intensity (Weiblen et al, 2015).

Harvest Metric

The next seed metric for rating seeds is the *harvest metric* which is rated as *grams of flower per plant*. This typically ranges from as low as 350 to as high as 600 grams per plant (Toonen et al., 2006). Similar to harvest per meters square is also the *harvest per plant* which can be a bi-seed analysis. Since auto-flowering plants tend to be shorter (since it's hard to actually manipulate them through photogenic cycles to grow them to be larger), the harvest per plant tends to be much smaller for auto-flowering plants than photogenic plants. For example, the harvest per plant in grams for an auto-flowering plant has a lower bound. It can range from 50 to 250 grams. However, for non-auto-flowering plants which can be manipulated and promoted to creating a greater harvest per plant, they grow up to a meter high which is great for indoor growing and can still have THC levels of up to 20%. Note that indoors, cultivators do not usually have the ability or the opportunity to grow plants to their maximum height, which could well exceed 10 feet. In this case you'll notice that the total biomass harvest per plant can be 700 grams per plant up to 2,000 grams per plant.

Cultivation Time Variable

A variable typically used for seed ratings is *cultivation time* which is the equivalent of growth time plus flowering time. This is typically rated between 65 days and up to 85 days, depending on the plant variety. Typically auto-flowering plants may be on the lower end but there's no rule when it comes to that.

Categorical Variables

Plants can also be analyzed by a series of *categorical variables*. These typically present as varying qualitative properties, like taste and aroma.

Taste and Aroma

This could include categories of citrus, earth/pine nuances, fresh menthol and floral, spices and musk, mint nuances, sweet notes and citrus fruits, earthy nuances and pine, mandarin and grapefruits, wood and elderberry, spicy, fruity, sandalwood, and many more.

Effect

This could include relaxing, narcotic, psychic effect, medical, powerful, onslaught, laughter, euphoria, psychedelic, cerebral, stress control, anxiety and mood improvement, as well as other factors.

Cycle

Plants that are not auto-flowering (or tend to grow outside with the natural outdoor growing cycle) will tend to go into full bloom and harvest either at the end of September and the end of October (from the standpoint of the Northern Hemisphere of the Earth).

Cultivation and the Earth: A Lens into the Soil and Water

Soil has many different and specific factors that affect how a seed grows. You have the option of using natural soil or soil that have been derived from compost (as one series of options available). This can be measured as either a *binary variable* or *categorical variable*. A *categorical variable* is similar to a binary variable, except there are more than two options. You also have natural supplements that can be added to the soil. Inputs can include worm castings, pH modifiers, and/or other nutrient additives that all contribute to growth conditions.

Nutrient Supplementation

Most growers buy an advanced growing nutrition supplement. They are typically prepackaged and sold at eight ounces or available in industrial sizes of 275 gallons for larger operations. These commercially available supplements simplify decision making for the grower by converting this complex input into a *binary variable* in exchange for a fixed (and higher) cost per unit.

Water

Water is a critical factor in plant growth, and must be closely monitored in different ways. The *pH level* relates both to soil and water. We know a pH of 7.0 is considered neutral. A lower pH is acidic and a higher pH is considered alkaline. The pH scale is a logarithmic scale that goes from 1 to 14. Since pH is measured on a logarithmic scale, it means that a pH of four is 10 times as acidic as a pH of five. A pH of three is 100 times as acidic as a pH of five. EPA recommendations limit typical tap water pH from 6.5 to 8.5, with variations based on minerals and dissolved carbon dioxide in the water supply.

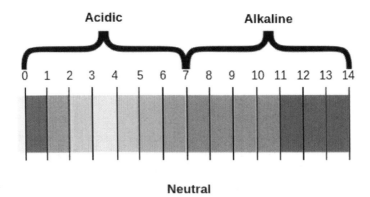

Illustration of pH Scale.

Soil versus Hydroponic

As far as the ranges for pH in soil, it depends on whether you're growing outdoors (in soil) or growing hydroponic (in a water-based, nutrient rich solution). If you're growing hydroponic, it's slightly more acidic than growing in soil. In soil you have a typical pH between 6.0 and 6.5, whereas in hydroponic it is a pH of 5.5 to 6.0.

pH Regulation and Measuring Soil Inputs

There are two different elements that can be used to help affect the pH and regulate it. If you want to raise the pH (make it more alkaline or basic), you can use a concentration of soluble potash which is potassium oxide at a 5.0% concentration. If you would like to bring the pH down, you could use a combination of nitrogen in concentration of 1.0% and phosphorous, P_2O_2 at a concentration of 5.0% in the solution.

Root Growth and Measuring Propagation

Without a proper root structure the plant will not reach its full capacity and may uproot itself with its own weight. Root growth is critical in the structure of the plant since it can grow very high. Thus we use a *rooting concentration* treatment in order to enhance what we call *propagation*. Typically, if a plant needs a soil nutrient to promote root growth, a cultivator will use a combination of indole-3-butyric acid (IBA) with a .07% concentration. They might also include NAA, a 1-naphthaleneacetic acid, that contains hormones and essential nutrients for promoting root growth within a plant (De Klerk et al., 1997).

Supplements and pH Regulation

The class of chemicals used to raise and lower the pH level are called supplements. Typically when you're looking at a complete nutrient solution you're going to see a name followed by a series of three numbers separated by dashes. If you see a name of a complete nutrient product followed by the numbers 7-8-6, this corresponds to the total nitrogen, phosphorus and potassium amounts by percentage in the chemical composition. Thus, if a nutrient solution claims to have 7-8-6 it means the total nitrogen is 7%, phosphorous or P_2O_5 is 8% and the potassium or K_2O is 6%.

Measuring and Monitoring the Big Three Macronutrients in Soil: NPK

Nitrogen (N) Soil Measurements

The bounded conditions for *nitrogen* tend to be on the low end of 3 and the high end of 7, and *total nitrogen* is actually the sum of two nitrogen components. One is ammonium (NH_4), another is nitrate (NO_3). The ratio of ammoniacal nitrogen to nitrate tends to be roughly 1:2, i.e. there is twice as much nitrate as there is ammoniacal.

Nitrogen is critical to the biosynthesis of the protein hormone chlorophyll (used in photosynthesis) and can influence other enzymes at work, which promotes stem and leaf growth. Too much nitrogen, however, can delay flowering. A deficiency in nitrogen can reduce yields, cause yellowing of leaves visually, and stunted growth (West et al., 2008).

Phosphorus (P)

Phosphorus is typically found in concentrations between 6% and 12%, while potassium tends to be optimally found between 5% and 7%. An all purpose formula will tend to have a relatively even ratio of nitrogen to phosphorus to potassium (7-7-7). However, you can trade off different chemical concentrations to give yourself a different desired effect (Brunings et al., 2012).

Potassium (K)

Potassium helps in the formation of sugars (carbohydrates) and proteins. You know you are dealing with potassium deficiency if you can see the leaf is spotted, curled, or has a burned look. Cultivators also find lower yields when deficiencies exist.

Micronutrients and other Minor Soil Compounds that Impact Plant Cultivation

In addition to the three primary macronutrients, nitrogen, phosphorus and potassium, there are about 13 other elements that are notable in nutrients. These include calcium (Ca), magnesium (Mg), sulfur (S), boron (B), chlorine (Cl), cobalt (Co), copper (Cu), iron (Fe), manganese (Mn), molybdenum (Mo), nickel (Ni), sodium (Na), and zinc (Zn).

Sulfur and boron tend to be two *orders of magnitude* less abundant in soil and plant material than magnesium with .05% and .2% respectively. An *order of magnitude* as a large multiple difference between two values. For example, 100 is an order of magnitude greater than 10, because it is 10 times larger than 10. On the other hand, 20 would not be considered an order of magnitude larger than 10 because it is only twice as large as 10.

If a cultivator is trying to create a plant with higher structure, they might also include potassium supplement, as well as *silicate*, which helps to reinforce the walls of the cell (Seifritz, 1990). This might be favorable for outdoor growing since silica is typically found in soils at a rate of 5 to 10 parts per million, you may require a supplement that increases that by an order of magnitude of 50 to 100 parts per million. As far as ratios go, if you want to encourage foliage and general plant growth, it is likely that you will be increasing the nitrogen concentration.

Causal Relationships versus Association Relationships

We mention all of this, because different formulas and compounds can be used at different parts of the plant growth stages for optimum performance. For example, early in the plant's life, you might find that formulas with low levels of nitrogen (but high in phosphorus), tend to promote flowering (this technique is helpful for growing vegetables and herbs). Flowering can also be encouraged through higher potassium levels.

You may notice these associations between variables in your bounded analysis, in what we call an *association relationship*, which is different than a *causal relationship* (Altman & Krzywinski, 2015). Association relationship means that we can see that two factors are correlated, and that one tends to occur, *on average*, at the same time as the other. A *causal relationship* is where we know that one factor directly causes the other factor to occur. For example, let's say we wanted to determine the relationship between what is going on with the weather, and the likelihood that it is raining. If we wanted to take a weak guess at whether it is raining or not, we can ask a question or take a measurement that is associated with rain, like "can I see clouds in the sky outside my window?" If it is cloudy, that may tell us that it is raining, because they are associated and tend to occur at the same time, but not all cloudy days yield rain. A causal relationship, a much stronger form of statistical relationship, is to ask "is it cloudy and do I see water falling past my window?" This implies that there may have been precipitation as a result of the clouds. However, please be aware that this does not guarantee that the water falling past your window means that it is raining: it could be cloudy outside at the same time that someone upstairs is spraying water past your window. All possibilities must always be considered.

On Average: A Magical Phrase in Statistics

An important realization about any mathematical, statistical, or computational model, is that they are all estimates. While data scientists do their best to create the most accurate estimates and predictions of effects as possible, it is important to know that the result is simply an average of many data points that is represented as a single value. That is why it is important in presenting statistical analysis to always try to emphasize that the results are being reported "on average".

Measuring and Monitoring Micronutrients in Soil: Other Elements on the Periodic Table

It's important to note that there are primarily two different types of nutrients in botany, grouped by their concentration rather than by their size. There are *macronutrients* and *micronutrients*. Macronutrients include nitrogen, potassium, calcium, magnesium, silicon, phosphorus and sulfur (Hawkesford et al., 2011). The micronutrients are iron, manganese, boron, zinc, chlorine, sodium, copper, molybdenum, cobalt and nickel. The typical threshold between a macronutrient and a micronutrient is a half percent, or .5% concentration level. Primary nutrients that enter the leaf are phosphorous, nitrogen, potassium, calcium, sulfur, silicon, and magnesium. For the root structure in the soil, you'll find boron, cobalt, iron, molybdenum, sodium, zinc, nitrogen, nickel, manganese and chlorine.

Calcium (Ca)

Calcium activates enzymes and is part of the structural wall of the cells, adding to the rigidity and strength of the plant. Calcium is also required for the uptake of nitrogen and other minerals. It's also important for continuous growth. You can tell if your plants are calcium deficient if you're stunting your growth and flowers and roots, or if you see black spots on the leaves or fruit, or yellowing leaf margins.

Calcium is unique in that its consistency across formulas remains at about a 2% level.

Magnesium (Mg)

Magnesium is critical to chlorophyll. If you're deficient in magnesium, you'll see yellowing between the veins of older leaves, signs of chlorosis, or leaves drooping. It can be leached by watering, and a foliar spray can correct the deficiencies (Bohn et al., 2006). Magnesium tends to be at a .5% level.

Silicon (Si)

Silicon is a macronutrient. It helps with the cell and the build of the cell walls as well, increases fertility, improves heat and drought tolerance resistance, and reduces transpiration (Luckx et al., 2017). You know if you're deficient in silicon if you see wilting, poor fruit or flower set, and also, increased susceptibility to insects and disease.

Sulfur and boron tend to be two *orders of magnitude* less than magnesium with .05% and .2% respectively.

Phosphorus (P)

Phosphorus is necessary for seed germination, and overall metabolism and growth. You know if you're deficient in phosphorus if there are purple stems and leaves, or if there's slow growth, as well as poor flowering. If your pH is too acidic or too low, it ties up the phosphates in the organic soils. But, if you increase phosphorus too much it can be toxic for the plant.

Sulfur (Su)

Sulfur is another macronutrient that can be identified as part of the amino acids that are necessary to the plant. You'll find that when there's deficiencies in sulfur, you'll see visually light green leaves, which can be leached by watering.

Iron (Fe)

Iron is important for enzyme functions and a catalyst for synthesizing chlorophyll and other new growth in the plant. If it's deficient, you'll find visually pale leaves as well as yellowing of the leaves and veins. It can be leached by water. It's possible to have high pH iron in the plants; however, if your pH is too high (in the iron in the soil), then it might be unavailable to the plant (Colombo et al., 2014).

Iron can be .07% up to .1%.

Manganese (Mn)

Manganese helps in aiding enzyme photosynthesis activity and respiration, and nitrogen metabolism. If you are deficient in manganese you'll have young leaves that have pale, green veins, similar to when iron deficiency occurs. In advanced stages, you're going to find brown, black, or gray spots next to the veins.

Manganese can be .05%.

Boron (B)

Boron is a micronutrient that can cause deficiencies in the soil. It affects 16 different functions of the plant, including flowering, pollen, generation, fruiting, cell division, water maintenance, membrane integrity, and movement of calcium and sugar. It's immobile and can be easily leached. Leaching is the loss of water-soluble plant nutrients from the soil, due to rain and irrigation.

Boron tends to be two *orders of magnitude* less than magnesium with .05% and .2% respectively.

Zinc (Zn)

Zinc is a functional part of the growth hormones of a plant, molted leaves, and irregular yellow areas are part of a zinc deficiency. Zinc deficiencies lead to iron deficiencies. It happens quite often in eroded soils.

Zinc can be .05%.

Chlorine (Cl)

Chlorine is involved in osmosis, or the movement of water into the cells. If you're low on chlorine you'll see wilting, stubby roots, yellowing and bronzing. It's leached by watering. The scent may also be decreased if there's a lack of chlorine.

Chlorine has a range of about .006 up to 01.006%.

Sodium (Na)

Sodium helps with the nitrogen metabolism in the plant and keeps ionic balance since it's a positive ion. A deficiency involves yellowing of the leaves and yellow tip burn, which may inhibit the flower formation.

Sodium can be .05% up to .1%.

Copper (Co)

Copper is found in the roots and necessary for nitrogen metabolism. You will typically see this definitely in highly organic soils, and the development of brown spots on terminal leaves. Copper can be .007% or .05%.

Molybdenum (Mo)

Molybdenum is good for the structural enzymes. It reduces nitrates to ammonia. It's critical for synthesis of proteins. Deficiency involves pale leaves with rolled and cupped margins.

Seeds may not form. If molybdenum is deficient, nitrogen may also be deficient in the soil.

Molybdenum can be .0009%.

Cobalt (Co)

Cobalt is required for nitrogen fixing, or incorporation of in-organic nitrogen into carbon-based (organic) molecules by soil bacteria (Dixon and Wheeler, 1983). It contributes to B12 and DNA biosynthesis. It may extend the life of cut flowers. But, also, lack of cobalt may cause a deficiency in available nitrogen because of its tendency to fix nitrogen.

Cobalt concentration in quality growing soil ranges from .0005% to .0015%.

Nickel (Ni)

Nickel has only recently been identified as an essential player within the botany world, and is required by seeds to germinate (Mishra and Kar, 1974).

Nickel is .001%.

Water and Irrigation: What is the Best Way to Manage Water?

As we already discussed, pH is a critical element in water, which relates directly to soil. However, what is also important to note about water, is that it must be cycled through the plant. Water and soil are companions, but soil cannot be too wet or too dry. Additionally, once added, water cannot overflow or create excess moisture (it must be removed as necessary).

We already discussed nutrients in the context of soil and cultivation. As we start talking more about plants, we'll notice that there's an important thing to note about *clones*, and how you can grow them in soiled environments or non-soiled environments. Clones can be rooted every 10 days in a full cycle. Growing clones indoors might have the advantage of not being subject to pests.

The binary variable involved in soils is the *soilless* versus *soil-rich* technology. Soil can be used for multiple purposes. In addition to worm casters, you can also make soil from compost. There are materials included in the plants within the mix being composted itself that can sustain it for one to two weeks, without degradation or the need for nutrients.

Flow Rate and Anti-Clogging Irrigation Geometry

The main metrics for water are: water in per day, water out per day, and gallons per hour (GPH). (Sharma et al., 2009). We use *GPH as our standard flow metric*. Ideally, when it comes to distribution of water, we want to provide a lower flow rate to evenly distribute water over a large filtration area, while, at the same time, maximizing what we call *turbulence*. From the perspective of a data scientist, working with these factors allows a grower to introduce other binary variables. We want to make sure that there is also clog resistance within the flows. Controlling the *likelihood of clogging* within a system could be another potential important variable. The importance of low flow rates impacts the grower's ability to use longer *lateral lengths* as part of the irrigation geometry, and maintain sub-main pipes, which results in higher savings in irrigation system costs (materials plus labor, or physical plus human capital). These percentages can range between 10-20%, and have a material cost on the production process, which can affect the price paid by the consumer (Tejero et al., 2014).

In a physical distribution system, we want conditions that are *ultra low*. Ultra low is 0.1 gallons per hour. Lower flow rate means longer pipe laterals and longer distribution, because if your pipe isn't leaking early on you can cover more area (meaning that you can distribute water down the entire pipe more readily). Typically, a drip is achieved by creating a mesh system in the pipe, coupled with a wide flow path, and a physical labyrinth structure within the pipe. These products can generally be used on an open row of field crops. To aid with this, there are *SDI applications* that are surface or subsurface. Subsurface means below the surface of the soil, and is calculated in *MILs* (MIL is the unit used for water distribution, and can range from 8 to 15). If you are looking at the different distributions, the depth range could typically be between 8 and 15 MIL (8 is the more shallow of the two).

Measuring Pipes and Irrigation Geometry

Water distribution planning also includes decisions about pipe systems and burial depth, which can range from being above the surface to shallow burial (shallow is considered to be up to 8" below the surface, and deep burial is considered to be up to 24" below). So the burial range can be from zero, through 8" to 24" for the pipes. Looking at a dripper (which distributes the water), the elements that typically must be evaluated, are *filtering area*, *MIL*, and the wall thickness of the pipes (the inside diameter of a pipe can range between 1/2" and 1.5").

Pressure Metrics

The next metric is *pressure*. Maximum pressure is reflected as a range for the two different types of pressure ranges, which are *operating pressure* and *flushing pressure*. The operating pressure tends to be between 12 and 32 psi, while the flushing pressure tends to be between 15 and 50 psi.

As far as the *nominal flow rate,* it is measured in gallons per hour (GPH), standardized at a test pressure of 10 psi (it can be as low as .11 gallons per hour, and up to .49 gallons per hour). It may also help to note *reel length* as a metric to evaluate. You can build the data model by looking at the *constant* and the *exponent* on the flow. The constant can be between .03 and .17, the exponent is almost always .45.

Filtration Mesh Geometry

The filtration mesh and dripper rate are correlated. Filtration mesh of 120 corresponds to a drip rate of .11 gallons per hour, whereas a filter mesh of 80 corresponds to .49 gallons per hour. The dripper flow code ranges between .1 and .5, for a flow rate of respectively .11 gallons per hour (and up to .49 GPH) (*Applied Engineering in Agriculture*, 2000).

Emission Uniformity and Water Dispersement Metrics

Another metric for evaluating the pipes is EU, or *emission uniformity*. This is measured as a percentage on a scale of either 90%, 92%, or 94%. That is over the length of the pipe. So as it increases in uniformity, there's higher demand on the pipe, less likelihood that it succeeds, or delivers a smaller result. A reasonable pipe can be as low as 500'. But, for a higher than 94% (from 12" up to 24"), the emission uniformity can be up to 2,000'.

Water distribution systems all have similar pieces. The four main pieces that they have are *filters* (which help to regulate flow rate), water quality, and clogging. *Valves* are manufactured from high quality materials, like nylon, PVC, iron, and bronze, and are required for superior hydraulic performance.

There can either be *straight flow* (which can also be characterized as low friction loss), or they can be *two-way valves*. PVC valves can have a higher resistance to corrosive water. Water meters help you get accurate flow readings, which is critical. You want to make sure that high quality and measurement of water, can be accomplished ultrasonically (through a double beam ultrasonic sensor).

Air Vents

Air vents are used to protect the irrigation system from any rupturing due to temperature or other pressure changes. If you have a properly vented irrigation system, it can extend the life of your drippers and prevent potential clogging. The air vents can be characterized as binary variables as either *vacuum relief, continuous acting*, or an *air vacuum event*. It could also be presented as a combination of the two.

Performance Analysis of Irrigation System

You should note that the slope of these pipes is standardized at 0% (meaning that they're on an even flat surface), when conducting performance analysis.

How do We Maintain the Biosecurity of Assets?

The use of biosecurity assets is another important discrete categorical variable, that should be documented by your system. Pesticides and similar types of products are regulated by the EPA and registered either as *disinfectants, virucides, fungicides, deodorizers, or food contact surface sanitizers* (EPA, 2019). Agricultural pesticides are typically sold in liquid formulations that can be easily transported, and allow a variety of convenient application methods (including a sprays, foams and fogs). What they're typically very helpful with is removing and decontaminating biofilms and tend not to contain Volatile Organic Compounds (VOCs).

Three-phase Administration Process of Biosecurity Assets and Fertilizers

Typically, these types of materials are administered in three phases:

1. *quaternary ammonium compound,*
2. *hydrogen peroxide,* and
3. *diacetin* (or a booster).

The quaternary compound has a boiling point of 200 Fahrenheit, and a freezing point of 26 Fahrenheit, with a pH that's very high (between 9.5 and 10.5). It typically has a pale yellow color with a sweet, soapy odor. In contrast, hydrogen peroxide has a 210 degree Fahrenheit boiling, 32 Fahrenheit freezing, and a pH that's very low. In concentrate, it can be built as low as 2 to 3, but once it's blended it comes out larger (9.6 or 9.9). Diacetin has a boiling point of 498 Fahrenheit, freezing point of -22 Fahrenheit, with no pH. It's also clear and odorless.

When applied to data science, flow rates and distribution (especially with fertilizers), can vary between one gallon per minute, and up to 100 gallons per minute. This is an example of a good *bounded analysis* range. Soil can also be measured in different categorical variables, as in the type of plug that is used to work with the plant.

Plugs and Filtration Screens

Note: There are typically either G plugs or Q plugs. Q plugs allow the grower to transplant large-rooted plants, and give you twice the turnaround in the same space. Recording these as a categorical variable can add a level of detail to your model.

From soil to how the complete grow system works with water filtration, there are different types of ways to maintain the water. You can either filter it through disc filtration, sand media filtration, screen filtration, and sand separation. Disc filtration has a small footprint and is a three dimensional filter that can remove organic contaminants. The sand media does a process of *back flush cleaning*. Screen filtration prevents coarse materials from entering a drip system, and minimizes maintenance by preventing clogging. Sand separation is good for pre-filtering water with high loads of sand passing through it.

Cultivation and the Greenhouse: Equipment and Greenhouse Metrics

"You want to have precise control over the lighting and purity of the environment from any bio-contaminates, which could negatively impact plant growth."

The ideal greenhouse infrastructure is a data-driven environment, that provides a consistent and repeatable yield, with uniformity, precision and full control over the growing environment. Ideally, the results of this would result in increased yields, streamlined workflow, reduced waste, and driving up the value of every crop cycle. This can be maintained by regulating and monitoring the integration of lighting, airflow, heat exchange, temperature, humidity control, CO_2 control, irrigation, and nutrient management.

Currently, there are many providers that sell turnkey solutions for greenhouses. A standardized indoor greenhouse, with a nine foot ceiling, will cost about $300 to $500 per square foot to set up (in total fixed costs). It should yield about a pound per year. Growth spaces typically come in several forms. The first is the tissue culture room (also known as the cloning rooms), where new seedlings and clones are cultivated before they're transferred into the main growing room or master greenhouse.

Standardized Green House Infrastructure Investment Metric: price per square foot.

Standardized Green House Infrastructure Yield Return Metric: price per square foot per year per pound of flower.

For greenhouses, you want to have precise control over the lighting and purity of the environment from any bio-contaminates, which could negatively impact plant growth.

Biocontamination is typically measured in parts per million.

Racks and benches are also important, since space is valuable in greenhouse structures. Optimally, you want to keep the geometry of your equipment to a minimal footprint. For the growing area, you'll want to have racks with standard weight rating of 20 pounds per square foot.

Standard rack weight rating, continuous variable: pounds per square foot.

Coupled with that, you may want to use a nanobubble generator (which is a new technology used to convert bulk oxygen into nanobubbles and supersaturate water with high levels of dissolved oxygen). The standard GPM flow rate is between 25 and 50 for this, and while the science has not yet come out on this technology, the elevated oxygen in the root zone level is supposed to enhance nutrient uptake, improve root mass, suppress pathogens, and support healthy vegetative flowering characteristics.

Oxygen rich nanobubble water can help to prevent root disease, reduce plant stress, shorten internode spacing, increase plant yield, remove biofilm, and prevent emitter blockages, all of which are desirable characteristics.

While building out your greenhouse infrastructure, there are other important auxiliary services that maybe very necessary for creating optimum growth conditions. These include analytical testing supplies, certified reference materials, chillers, temperature control systems chromatography supplies, decarboxylation and vacuum ovens, fume hoods that clean air, safety equipment, milling equipment, quality control solutions, rotary vapors, sample prep equipment, short path distillation solvents, reagents, as well as terpenes formulations and vacuum pumps.

The Clone Room

In the *tissue culture room*, or the *clone room*, what typically happens is you'll want a nominal system that's about 240 square feet, or 10 by 24 feet, to house cloning.

Cloning room size: square feet

Cloning room concentration: jars per square foot

Closing room light intensity: micromoles per meter

Cloning room temperature range: interquartile range of celsius [25% percentile, 75% percentile]

The standard jar for a clone should be a three-inch jar. About 6,000 jars fit in 240 square feet, leaving space for about 20 jars per square foot. The other important thing is light intensity. It's measured in *micromoles per meter squared per second*. The temperature in the tissue culture room should be between 15 and 30 degrees Celsius and minimized to no more than one degree Celsius of volatility to control.

Cloning room relative humidity: interquartile range of relative humidity [25% percentile, 75% percentile]

In the clone room, you want your maximum relative humidity, with the lights on, to be 75%, but since it's easier for humidity to be in cold air, with the lights off, the maximum relative humidity should be 90% instead of 75%. The standard lighting is a fluorescent bulb, and the clear shelf height should be about 20 inches. As far as scaling up to a multipurpose growing room from the clone room, the production scale rooms tend to abide by a ratio of eight mother plants per four foot by eight foot bench, or 32 flowering plants per four foot by eight foot bench. For the multipurpose growing room, about 10 by 24 (6,000 jars), which translates to 1,000 clones, or 48 mother plants, and 2,500 plants in a vegetative state. The ratio grows from there.

Introduction of Interquartile Ranges as Cannabis Metrics and Making Better Investment Decisions

In the previous section you may have noticed interquartile ranges being introduced as a concept for measurement. The reason relates to the type of metrics we have now introduced in our data pipeline. Metrics are great snapshots of the state of a situation: a single, fixed data point, that can describe what is happening at a given point in time. Examples of single data point metrics are the number of jars in the room, because they can be counted and summed to a single value. However, what happens if the nature of the value being reported does not take the shape of a single point, but rather a wave? Sinusoidal waves are commonly observed in measurements that are part of cycles, or that alternate between a range, like temperature or relative humidity. It is almost impossible to control the actual temperature in the room to an exact point, especially because the temperature itself is a measurement of averages (the average thermal energy in an object or space). It is not impossible, per se, but the equipment required to maintain the exact temperature in a room is actually very expensive, because it is a difficult problem to solve. Additionally, the plant doesn't need to be subject to an exact temperature to grow: outdoor environments and forests experience temperature swings through all four seasons of the year.

That is why we find the temperature range that the plant will grow within, and we optimize our equipment acquisition function to tell us exactly how much we should be paying in order to keep the temperature within the range that we want. This way, we don't pay for more precision in our equipment's performance than is required, preventing us from passing the cost downstream to the consumer.

Production Room Ratios and Metrics

Flower to Mother Plant Ratio: count of flower plants divided by count of mother plants. Ideally, about 15 to 20.

Looking at production scales, a 20 foot by 36 foot room gives you 28 mother plants and 512 flower plants. Whereas, a 30 foot by 68 foot room gives you space for 384 mother plants and 1,536 flower plants. If you're going to set up a drying room, you'll note that the drying ratio tends to be 25% of wet weight, and it takes about 10 to 14 days to dry (depending on loading, trimming and strain). If you want to look at the ratio, an 8 foot by 16 foot drying room can produce about 120 pounds, whereas a room with dimensions 12 foot by 32 foot yields 480 pounds in dry weight.

Small Grow Operations versus Large Grow Operations

Until now, we have primarily been discussing mass production, or large grow operations. Another *binary variable* is to record *whether the grow operation is considered "Large" or "Small"*. This will help highlight other factors you may need to measure and take into consideration. For smaller grow operations, you should look at different types of containers. Containers for plants can range from .25 to 25 gallon containers.

Container Size per pot: gallons per container pot (double variable)

Stakes per pot: count per container pot (integer)

You also want to consider the stakes. If you want a one-gallon pot or small container, it requires one stake per pot (for support). A three-gallon pot would require two stakes. A five to seven container is four stakes. A 10 to 25 gallon container up to six stakes. The stakes are used for spraying. Typically, the spray stakes are PC stakes, or pressure compensation stakes. To get flow between these stakes, they typically require at least 30psi. If we were to create a categorical metric for the size discrepancies between a small room versus a large grow room, let's say that a small room, typically, would be characterized as less than 10,000 feet. And for commercial operations, you would anticipate seeing anywhere between 10,000 and 50,000 square feet indoors.

Total Operation Size, indoor: square feet

Total Operation Size, outdoor: acres or hectares

Cultivation and Light: The Mathematics of Lighting

"Lighting in the cannabis cultivation process can be thought of in five separate stages: Mother Plant Cultivation, Cloning, Clone Implantation, Vegitative, and Flowering."

In How Many Ways Does Light Impact Growth?

Lighting is one of the most critical factors for yield and outcomes of a plant. Lighting not only determines yield, but it also dictates the schedule through which the *vegetative* and *flowering* states occur. Unless a plant is out of flowering, it will be photogenic, because then it will respond to the light cycles as required.

Vegetative State: the early part of a plant's growth cycle where the plant is preparing to flower and dedicating its energy toward the supporting structure like roots and stalks.

Flowering State: the latter part of a plant's growth cycle where the plant is flowering, and has dedicated its energy toward growing flowers and buds.

A plant will vegetate and grow to enhance its ability to reproduce and survive to the next generation. In cannabis cultivation, this is for the first half of the growing cycle. After cloning, the plant goes through a vegetative state where it grows its primary structures before flowering to enhance its capacity to yield buds.

The vegetative state occurs during a light cycle that lasts 18 hours on, 6 hours off. This is because the plant tries to guess what season it is currently growing in by measuring the amount of light it receives, where 18 hours of sunshine is indicative of a standard summer season schedule. At the summer solstice (the longest day of the year, June 21st), there are about 18 hours of light and 6 hours of darkness. However, as the season starts to get cold, the plant needs to reproduce (to survive through the cold winter). It will start flowering to produce seeds, and reproduce itself. The plant knows to do this because it sees the seasons change due to the change it senses in the light cycles. When we approach the Autumn equinox and flowering, it shifts the lighting ratio resulting in 12 hours of darkness and 12 hours of light.

Vegetative Lighting Ratio: Hours per day On to Hours per day Off, e.g.. 18:6 . Both values must add up to 24 in order for the metric to be valid.

Flowering Lighting Ratio: Hours per day On to Hours per day Off, e.g.. 12:12 . Both values must add up to 24 in order for the metric to be valid.

Modeling the Geometry of Light Angles

The geometry of light angles is less of an issue for indoor growing, because the cultivator is able to design exactly how they want the light to hit the plant.

However, if you are cultivating outside, due to the tilt of the earth, and the changing seasons, you may have to run a model on your longitude and latitude to determine exactly what your flowering schedule should be. Additionally, the tilt of the earth matters because it affects not just the intensity of light that reaches the plant, but also the wavelengths of light (more to come in the next sections). A more direct angle allows for the smaller wavelength blue lights to reach the plant, while a wider angle allows only the larger wavelength red light to reach the plant. To imagine this simply, just visualize a sunset. The point at which the angle between you and the sun is the least direct, which is why sunsets are red.

Lighting Directness: angle difference, as measured from directly at zero degrees.

Lighting Obstruction: the average daily percentage of light that enters the atmosphere but does not reach the plants on the ground.

Lighting Intensity: the percentage of light, relative to the seasonal maximum, that is being received by the plant. This is a product of the average sunlight intensity, the lighting directness, and (1 minus the percentage of lighting obstruction).

Cultivation: The Stages of Plant Growth and Lighting

Lighting in the cannabis cultivation process can be thought of in five separate stages: Mother Plant Cultivation, Cloning, Clone Implantation, Vegetative, and Flowering.

Stage 1 (Mother Plant): The mother plant should display strong vegetative growth and good branching, to enable higher production and higher quality cuttings. Because, after all, the clones are cut from the mother plant.

Stage 2 (Cloning or Tissue Culture Stage): The tissue culture stage is where clones are made. In this type of environment, ideally, there are low measurements of bio-contaminants like mold, pests and bacteria (during what we call the *micropropagation process*). At this point, we encourage higher frequency blue lights and lower UVA wavelengths. By encouraging strong plants and helping them resist outside contaminates, we observe a higher survival rate, which will result in stronger plants (both structurally and in their production in the third stage). During cloning, we want to keep a relatively low humidity, maintain a contaminate-free environment and a light distribution that is uniform among the clones.

Average Wavelength of Stage 2 Lighting: measured in nanometers.

Tissue Culture Survival Rate: percentage of clones that survive from start to implantation. Sudden drops in this value may be an indicator of other issues in your greenhouse.

Stage 3 (Clone Implantation): The clones may be ready to be transferred out of the tissue culture room, but still may not have the root structure to stand in soil on its own. This is where additional nutrients and time are fed to the plant to grow its basic infrastructure before being transferred into the greenhouse with the vegetative plants.

Stage 4 (Vegetative): During the vegetative stage, plants tend to be compact and slim, which helps with this idea of vertical farming. Although the plants may be small, they will eventually be ripe to flower.

Stage 5 (Flowering): For each flowering plant, you want to measure the quality and the chemotype after each cycle. Taking frequent measurements helps us to anticipate the amount of dry flower weight, as well as an increased concentration in cannabinoids, like THC and CBD (Smith et al., n.d.).

When looking at light intensity, the *PPFD is measured in micromoles per meters squared per second*, as previously stated. This can alternate in intensity by a range of between 50 and 800 PPFD. When you're working with a mother plant, the PPFD is typically 400, which is actually similar to that of the vegetative stage. You want to maintain a lamp height of about 12 inches above the mother plant. Once you prune the mother plant for a tissue culture, you want to lower the intensity down to 50 micro-moles per meter squared per second. You also want to raise the light height to about 16 inches above the plant.

Output per light tube: about 25 micromoles per meters squared per second.

You raise the intensity of the light at each stage of growth. Even though, by the end of the flowering stage, the light will be on for less time, it will also be at its most intense. From tissue culture to cloning stage, you go from a PPFD of 50 to a PPFD of 140, but then you physically lower the light closer to the plant (to about 12 inches). For the vegetative stage, after the plant is past cloning and tissue culture, you can turn up the intensity of the light to 400 PPFD. For the first half of the vegetative stage you'll keep the light at about 10 inches from the plant. Then, later in the vegetative stage, you'll raise it to two feet, depending on the bulb and orientation. There's also a graphical analysis of how you can layout the intensity of the different lights and how you can orient them. You can either have them spaced uniformly or have them separated. By the time you reach the flowering stages, your PPFD will be close to 800 PPFD and your plants will be exposed to light at a distance of anywhere between six inches and two feet above the plant.

As far as the type of light and the spectrum that helps promote different types of growth, you know that deep blue radiation creates a healthy stress in the plant and can help encourage high cannabinoid concentrations. Along with small amounts of UVA, both trigger development of more cannabinoids. How this UVA implementation is measured is up to speculation and worth evaluating. When it comes to light spectrum data, as far as the aggregate light goes, there are a few different measures you can use. Here are some measures to consider:

-One is CCT or Correlated Color Temperature (analogous to "Kelvins"), which in this case, is about 4600.

-The CRI, which is the *color rendering index*, is about 95 (very high). CRI is the degree to which object colors render naturally under a light source.

-The "B to G" ("Blue to Green") ratio is about .8, and the R to FR ("Red to Far Red") ratio is about 14.

-As far as spectrum data on the remaining, you have about 1% in ultraviolet light (which is less than 400 nanometers), 24% is blue (at 400 to 500 nanometers wavelength), green is 34% (at 500 to 600 nanometers), red is 38% (at 600 to 700 nanometers), then the far red spectrum is 3% (at 700 to 800 nanometers).

The different types of bulbs are standardized as either HPS bulbs or LEDs. Historically, mercury bulbs and metal halide bulbs have been used at different stages (depending on if you want red lights or blue lights). However, the LED lights tend to outperform the HPS lights by nearly a factor of two. Light inputs can vary from 120 to 240 volts, and even have higher industrial inputs of up to 277 VAC. or *volts of alternating current* (discussed more in the next section). Ultimately, what you want is a *full spectrum* light that captures everything in your space.

You also want to measure the ambient temperature of the lights as they operate, which can vary from zero degrees Celsius all the way up to 40 degrees Celsius. This is important when providing calculations for temperature management in the space.

Cultivation and Air: When Do You Need CO_2 Supplementation?

Without supplementation, the normal CO_2 level in air is 400 parts per million (0.04%). With CO_2 sublimation, you can see up to 800 to 1400 parts per million, which is especially helpful during reproductive growth stages of the plants due to high PPFD levels.

Cultivation and Electricity: Maintaining Ideal Temperature and Air Conditions

What Does 'Correct Voltage' Mean?

The voltage from lights can go from 120 VAC all the up to 347 VAC. We want to understand a little about power input, which is measured in *watts*. This can be as low as 100 all the way up to 400 watts. You will want to measure the current input on the lights, to determine how much power is necessary. It can be as low as 0.4 amps all the way up to 2 amps. The light output, which can be as low as 300 micromoles per second all the way up to 880 or 900 will affect this. The *light efficiency*, which is measured in *micromoles per watt*, is typically between 2.0 and 3.0 micromoles per watt. Ultimately, the light cycles will happen between vegetative, growth and flowering stages. The three main light types that you typically use are 5000K full spectrum white light (a Vegemax), which can replace a fluorescent or a metal halide (which is MH light). These lights traditionally output a high level of blue light, which is comparable to strong light in the summer.

The color temperature of the vegetative light is the same as the midday sun, with a high level of blue content (which is what correlates to the 25% in total PAR). What this does is prevent stretching of the plants and ensures intense leaf development, strong root growth, and shorter internodal distance.

PAR is Photosynthetic Active Radiation: watts per meter squared.

Internodal distance is the distance between the growth sprouts and the branches: meters.

As we start moving from the vegetative stage to the growth stage, we can move from a 5000K full spectrum white light to a

4000K Kelvin intensity (both kept under low profiles, could be between one and two feet away from the plant). For the 4000K spectrum light, the light temperature is between those of the sun, and a tungsten filament light. It has a strong blue profile as well as a peak in red. It can be used for an entire plant cycle, if you don't want to separate out the vegetative and flowering stage. It's a good mid-range pick and is really helpful for auto-flowering plants.

Once we're in the flowering stages, we might use a 3000 Kelvin normalized photo flux light, which has a color temperature of the spectrum that is particularly high in levels of red (indicative of the sun being lower to the horizon. Since the light has to pass through more of the atmosphere in order to reach us, it gets more filtered, so we get more of a red light. This high level red content is correlated to 44% of the total PAR. It helps increase photosynthetic efficiency and creating high yields.

In a fascinating parallel, guidelines for installing lights of different Kelvin ratings within human occupied spaces is very similar to that for plants. Offices and kitchens where work and productivity are occuring, a parallel to a plant's vegitative state, tend to have white lights with Kelvin ratings at about 5000. However, industry recommendations of lighting within human living spaces and bedrooms is about 3000 K. Thus, we see a parallel between plants and humans where productive spaces have lighting at 5000 K, while plants and humans also tend to have their reproductive spaces filled with lighting at 3000 K.

PAR efficiency is measured up to 2.6 micromoles per joule, and the power also varies between the vegetative bulbs, the grow bulbs, and the flower bulbs. It increases in power, even though it decreases in spectrum. The vegetative bulbs are 200 watts nominal power. The grow bulbs are 300 watts, and the flower bulbs are 600 watts. An appropriate IP rating and certification to look for is an IP 63.

HVAC: What is the Current Suggested Best Management of HVAC System and Grow Room?

In-depth planning of a facility, determining the loads, and correctly sizing the climate system in advance are important for keeping your costs low. Here, we will look at some maintenance factors. In the industrial indoor cultivation facilities, you may face very unique and difficult challenges that impact your indoor climate control and HVAC systems. Constant measurement of this system is a key aspect to understanding how everything is performing in real time. An HVAC system in a grow room helps you figure out how to manage your botanical processes, thermal dynamics, fluid dynamics, support systems, lighting, and dehumidification (in order to provide climate control). Plants need to breath and an indoor climate system must react to changing SHR requirements. Sensible heat or cooling loads are divided by the total sensible heat, which is sensible plus latent or the cooling loads.

Modeling Vapor Pressure Deficit

Another metric used for determining grow room conditions, especially in indoor farming, is a term called *vapor pressure deficit* (VPD). Transpiration is how a plant breathes through its leaves, or better said, the plant's use of water to carry nutrients through the tissues and release this water as vapor via tiny openings in the plant's surfaces (called stomata) to the surrounding area. Since plants rely heavily on water and create food during photosynthesis, approximately 99% of the water delivered to the plant's root actually travels up into the plant before passing through stomata to become water vapor (or risk becoming a latent load that must be controlled). The natural plant process will facilitate it.

The plant is actually helping to facilitate the humidity in the room. Thus, it is important for us to control vapor and remove it as required. In order to measure the VPD, we use a *moisture load calculation*. We model this to find the *vapor pressure differential*. The standard way of determining moisture load in a grow room is to calculate the net water usage of plants. In theory, you should be able to just measure it by looking at the volume of your irrigation water used in the grow room less the volume that exits down from drainage. The difference is the volume of moisture that is transpired or evaporated from plants. However, you'd have to require an irrigation system to be actually active while measurement devices are recording. This, from a data science perspective, creates an endogeneity problem.

Endogeneity Problem in measurement: the problem of accurately measuring because the act of measurement itself may distort the final reading.

Penman-Monteith Formula

What has typically been used in industry is a model called the *Penman-Monteith formula* (Moran et al., 1996). It can also be used for indoor and outdoor grow environments to estimate *evapotranspiration*. It can look at the combination of evaporation and plant transpiration processes, where the water alternates in state between gas and liquid. The important thing to note about the formula, is that it generates a reference crop value that estimates the moisture released per day for a large field of a uniform crop. To generate a reference crop value for indoor grow rooms, the formula uses a shortwave radiation value of 1.53 MJ per meters squared each hour during the "lights on" period.

The value of 1.53, to generate a reference crop value for indoor grow rooms, is approximately equal to 50% of the sun's daily value shortwave radiation at the equator. Other key variables used in the calculation are net radiation, design air temperatures, velocity of ventilation air (at a level of three feet above

Nima Veiseh

the plant canopies), and VPD differentials. Additional key variables that impact evaporation are the actual crop canopy size at full growth (measured in square feet), the space temperature, and the humidity levels. The number of lights and hours of lighting are all individual variables that need to be accounted for, as well.

Plant Formation

There are two canopy stages where you check the form of your plants. One is low canopy, where the individual plant crowns are not yet matured in a shorter stage of development. The other is the high canopy stage when the crops are mature and at peak height. Typically, the plants can be trained or managed by netting that is involved, although netting should not typically be understood to have any effect on the product. It does help as a proxy for surface area, which is an important factor, because it allows for light distribution across the plants to be maximized.

Sensible Heat Ratio

The *sensible heat ratio, or* SHR is kept moderately high or greater than .75 SHR, if you have low canopy plants. A high sensible heat ratio can be achieved with almost any typical air conditioning unit. However, once a plant grows to a high canopy state, the evaporative cooling effects of transpiration will be high and sensible cooling requirements will be greatly reduced. This is because the plants use ambient heat in the room to convert water into vapor through transpiration.

In the "lights on" high canopy scenario, you want to design a SHR for air conditioning units that is medium to high at about 0.5 SHR to 0.6. Typical air conditioning units can help with this, however, without the units operating, the latent moisture loads will increase. In the "lights off" mode, the same problem occurs as with low canopy plants.

Relative Humidity

Relative humidity (RH) is a key factor in determining the success of a plant. Relative humidity is a measure of the amount of moisture in the air compared to what the air can sustain at a given temperature. Thus, relative humidity is a function of temperature. Cannabis growers can typically develop strategies to manage humidity at each stage of the growth. As previously discussed in our five-stage model, we typically want to manage the relative humidity in several ways. When we are initially propagating plants (in other words, when we are cloning them), the plants are at their most vulnerable stages. They require a high amount of humidity and consistent temperature, because you don't want them to dry out (especially with young roots that have yet to take hold in the soil and propagate). These young clones entirely rely on the humidity in the air to get their water from the leaves.

Next, when the plants are in their vegetative states, you can lower the humidity, and slightly increase the temperature to boost metabolic activity. In their vegetative state there will be a lot of light, because the plants think they're in summer, and the longer daylight cycles will help the plants establish root mass, as well as biomass, before they end in the flowering stage. Once the plant is ready to enter the flowering (or blooming process), the plant is triggered by the shorter light-cycle and reduced temperatures. The flowers start to develop the resins that ultimately contain the THC and CBD. Humidity should also be gradually lowered at this stage to prevent mold, mildew and other bio-contaminants from affecting the plant (Bassani et al., 2009).

After these final stages of plant maturation you want to dry the buds. For this you need to have high ventilation, and a low humidity environment, which will reduce the mass and the trichomes in the cannabis buds. During this phase, you remove unwanted pigment, chlorophyll, and prevent mold from forming on the leaves.

To summarize these considerations regarding humidity: When you're dealing with mother plants at the very beginning in propagation stage, you want the relative humidity to be 15% to 17%. In the propagating plants and clones stage you want between 80% and 90%. Tissue culture, where the tissue may be in solution after cloning, is best performed between a relative humidity of 60% to 70%. During the vegetative growth stage you can also start lowering the humidity (in the young plants) to around 50% to 70%. As the blooms start developing, the plant begins to flower, requiring the reduction of humidity to somewhere between 40% or 60%. When you're drying and curing the plants, you want the humidity to be between 45% and 55%.

Temperature Regulation

Another important maintenance factor for grow room environmental controls is temperature regulation. The important thing to note in looking at temperature versus relative humidity is that they're related (or functions of each other). Beware that *relative humidity* is often a misapplied term. It is used in place of the word, *absolute humidity*. The key is the word "relative." As the air temperature increases, the total volume of the air molecules increases and starts to spread out. Conversely, when air temperatures decrease the volume of the air molecules decreases, that is, the molecules start to be closer together, the air is denser.

However, unlike air, water is not compressible. Therefore, given a specific amount, it will always occupy the same amount of volume. As moisture in latent air is heated or cooled the air volume changes, but the amount of moisture in the air does not. This is important to understand, because water condensation occurs at an absolute humidity concentration, regardless of its relative humidity. This is known as the *constant dew point temperature*, and is the key metric in creating vapor pressure deficits for healthy plant growth.

Relationship of Temperature and Humidity

It is important to also be looking at in standardized systems is the relation between temperature and relative humidity. Typically, this can be modeled in machine learning or any sort of statistical analysis as a *time series*. A time series analysis is an analysis that looks at data over a particular time interval. Time series models are defined by three properties, trend, seasonality and cycle. Trend is the long run increase in a time series line. Seasonality are the cycles that raise and lower with a regular pattern over time. Cycle is like Seasonality except doesn't happen at a regular interval.

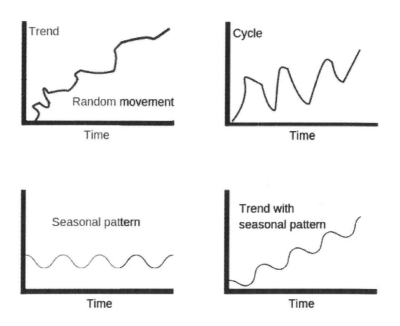

Illustrations of Time Series Terminology.

What you'll notice is that temperature volatility tends to be very high during a "lights off" period, as well as relative humidity (during that same period). You want to monitor this because if transpiration rates get too high this can cause unhealthy conditions and lead to wilting of the leaf or *tip burn*. To keep healthy transpiration rates and prevent this, it is important to provide *control vapor pressure differentials* as well as stable temperature conditions. If air is not being directed in flow across the plants, the condensation of leaves does not occur and it creates conditions for mold and fungi growth. Air directed at the plant leaves should be at temperatures above the designed dewpoints (Chandra et al., 2017).

There are four primary types of systems that you could use to manage the humidity and air conditioning in the space.

- conventional air conditioner with supplemental portable dehumidification units
- conventional air conditioning unit with enhanced dehumidification
- conventional air conditioning with a split dehumidification systems
- fully integrated environmental control system.

HVAC Energy Use

Air conditioners will typically use between 40 and 70 kilowatt hours (kWh), a dehumidifier at 9 to 24 kWh. Total energy, for "lights on", will be between 40 and 100 kWh. With "lights off" energy being between 16 and 40 kWh, a reduction of about 70%.

One of the other key metrics to utilize in terms of kilowatt hours is the *annual kilowatt hours per square foot consumed,* which can range between 65 on the lower bound up to 115 on the upper bound (Mills, 2012). Another key metric is the electric cost per year in square foot, which roughly goes between $7.80 up to $13.80 (Mills, 2012). Ultimately, what you want to do is look at the *impact of your real estate.* If you want to look at grow room total HVAC energy, you can create a graph (Perez-Lombard et al., 2011). On the X-axis is latent load or evapotranspiration. Latent load is measured in gallons per day per square foot. On the Y-axis is energy expended, which ranges between 50 and 200 kilowatt hours per square foot.

At this point in the system, the relative humidity is related to the irrigation expended and the flow rate of the irrigation. Latent dehumidification can be measured in *BTUh* (which ranges between 3,000 and 6,000), or pound hours (which is between 3.0 and 6.0), or latent operational kilowatts (which is between 0.6 and 0.9). The typical standard used for electricity in these tests, is at $12 per kilowatt hour. The canopy area for this calculation is standardized at 2600 square feet and a watering rate of 0.5 gallons per day per plant, or 0.15 gallons per day per square foot. The latent load is based off of the standard at 50 watts per square foot.

One of the latest measures to observe with portable dehumidifiers is the AHAM rating (or AHAM of 2.7 liters per kilowatt hour). Another key metric is the watering conversion rate, which is from gallons per day per square foot, to gallons per day per plant. These are all available. If you're using the metric of square foot per plant, it can range between 0.1 all the way up to 0.3.

Dehumidification can be measured in a graph for checking and comparing capacity. On the X-axis you have the water removal per hundred pounds per hour. Whereas, then on the Y-axis you have power unit kilowatts. You'll notice that the input for air is slightly higher than the input for water and we expect that, because water does a better job of moving heat. Also, as far as dehumidification goes, it might be helpful to *measure the compressor in horsepower (HP)*. The other efficacy issue with moisture removal, is to measure it in pounds per hour.

Air and Heat Circulation

Another input to measure, since ventilation is critical to cannabis cultivation, is circulation of air, heat and their respective distributions. Greenhouses have to be optimized through the movement of air through the space. What does a fan help do? Fans create an active microclimate at the crop level, resulting in a uniform climate in the greenhouses. It helps to control and regulate humidity, keeping a constant low airspeed to crop level, and reduces your energy costs through the vertical air-flow.

The amount of energy required to convert liquid water into vapor is approximately 1,060 BTUs per pound of liquid water. And in grow room terms, 2,600 watts of heat are needed to vaporize each gallon of water. The process, important to note for data scientist's metrics and modeling, requires approximately 50% of grow room light, heat output to complete the conversion. This means that 5,200 watts of lighting would vaporize one gallon of water per hour. Thus, this results in a gallon per day watering rate estimate, when your lights are on for 12 hours (which is during the fall season) your light wattage is 325, versus 18 hours where it is about 260.

Pascals and HectoPascals

Other units used for VPD are pascals, or hecto pascals. As you noticed, at the ideal growth stages, the temperatures at each stage matters. You have at the cloning stage, the vegetation, early flowering, and late flowering stages, a temperature that goes between 70 and 78 Fahrenheit. Then, we see relative humidity that drops from 80 to 50 and VPD that rises from zero up toward 1.5 KPA. As far as watering, it actually alternates. Initially in the clone stage you want saturated soil. Then in medium (during vegetative for that early flowering), you want to fill the area with water. Then during late flowering you want to start to dry out and preserve samples.

After drying the product for four to seven days at a relative humidity of about 50% and lower temperature, you want to cure it. The optimum temperature for this is between 15 and 25 degrees Celsius, with a humidity of 40% to 48%. A *wet load, or full harvest weight,* can go between 900 pounds and 3,000 pounds. Resulting in dry weight respectively of 180 to 600 pounds of flower.

What Types of Chillers Can Be Used?

Another important section is the idea of a chiller in the system. *Chillers are measured, typically, in size of tons, or tonnage.* And the compressors can either be single circuit, dual circuit or variable speed versus single speed (and recorded as a categorical variable). There are many different types of chillers. The chillers are typically in five different types. First type is an *air cooled scroll*. It comes in the form of the single or dual circuit and comes in tonnage of one to 170 tons. There is an *air cooled screw*, which is 130 to 470 tons and is adapted for variable speeds. The third type of chiller is a *water cooled screw*. It can go to a much larger scale from 70 to 800 tons. It has both single and variable speed compressors. The fourth type of chiller is a *water cooled centrifugal*, which goes much higher, from 300 to 4,000 tons, the largest volumes. This has a single stage or dual stage compressor. The fifth one is the *water cooled mag bearing centrifugal*, which is all variable speed. In addition to chillers, you'll find air handling units in the range a unit of CFMs. This is cubic feet and the CFM range is on the low side (about 1,000 or in nominal tons at 400 FPM - that's four tons). On the high end you have an air handler that has a CFM of 56,000.

Moisture Content Analysis

When weighing dry cannabis, it typically still has a moisture content of about 10% to 12%. Packaging, weighing, and dehydration regulation systems can affect the weight of a product by up to 2.5%, which could make a difference in the ultimate sale price, once it turns into a final product. Anything at 12% moisture is prone to mold growth (McKernan et al, 2016). This can be identified by doing a mycotoxins analysis.

Technical Substitution for Human Capital and Step Functions

One of the biggest advances in the cannabis industry in the next 20 years will be the introduction of technologies that replace the need for human labor. Although we are already seeing technological advances that allow us to produce and process on unprecedented scales, humans are still manually performing many tasks, like visually checking plants and trimming the crops. Some companies, like Bloom Automation, are innovating in the cannabis space by transferring technologies used in other parts of agriculture (i.e. Strawberry harvesting), to robotically trim cannabis plants (Stoll, 2019). Similarly, image recognition equipment and software is going to help monitor the health of plants without the necessary aid of human labor. This is an important consideration when thinking about capital investments and how future infrastructure will be put into place. Technical substitution for human capital has been an ongoing inevitability since automation took over the assembly lines of the automotive industry through the 20th century. At each of these moments of infrastructure advancement, we see what is called a *step function* change, or sudden shift in the return a model provides.

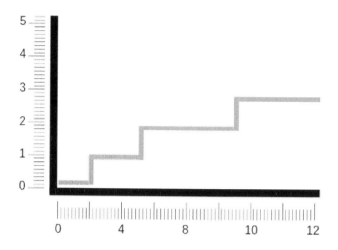

Illustration of Step Function.

Step functions are unique and important for our discussion for two reasons. First, they are not continuous linear functions, so can not be modeled like a normal linear regression function. They have a break in them, or *discontinuity*, that often results in a sudden rise or drop in a value being measured. Since they are not often used and can create a layer of complexity in a model, they are often ignored or missed completely. That leads us to the second point. Step functions are important because models that often get misread, especially models trying to understand growing industries or new phenomena, could have been better modeled with the use of a step function. For example, if we are trying to predict the number of plants that a robot can handle per hour, it will likely be low, until someone comes along and invents a breakthrough process for speeding up processing time. The problem is that if we are trying to predict how many more plants are being processed after the technological breakthrough, we run the risk of under-estimating if we use a continuous linear model. Step functions or radical technological improvements are also much more likely to happen in a nascent industry. Thus, it is important when looking at opportunities, policy changes, paradigm shifts and technological advances in an industry, to consider the possibility that we are approaching a step function in our model.

Hemp Product Possibilities and Environmental Sustainability

"Since the hemp plant is so versatile and resilient and requires less resources to grow in unstable environmental conditions, it is a strong candidate for filling industrialized needs in the least advantaged geographies on earth."

The hemp plant is one of the most versatile and useful plants known to scientists (Small & Marcus, 2002). After drying and processing it, there are many problems that the plant can be used to solve, from sustainability to medicine to opportunities in Corporate Social Responsibility, and many economic opportunities as well.

What Do You Do with the Dry Product? Answer: Everything.

Once the plant is grown, we use *hammer mills* to chop it up. There are several mills that you can use, similar to how grains or coffee would be prepared for transportation. The hammer mill produces fine to medium ground product. It can be used for hemp, newer grains, and wood shavings. The motors can be between 3 and 400 horsepower, depending on your needs. The important thing to note while using a hammer mill is that you should be looking at the capacity (it has a horsepower rating), which is pounds per hour. You should consider the screen size (which is the filtering section) and the number of hammers that it operates with. The number of hammers could range anywhere between 10 and 150 (Perez-Lombard et al, 2010).

Pellet Mills

Similarly, *pellet mills* (smaller machines) can take any number of things and produce pellets. The capacity is also in pounds per hour and can range as low as 30 or as high as 30,000 pounds per hour. The pellets produced need to be cooled. To do that, we use pellet coolers. The main metric for pellet coolers is capacity per hour. They can range between 100 pounds up to 20 tons per hour. This is very effective in processing biomass.

Pellet Crumblers

Now, *pellet crumblers* are designed to break the smelt (the pellets) back into a consumable product, and these have low motor ratings of three to 10 horsepower. The roll dimensions, flanged end feed dimensions, flanged out feed dimensions, and the total dimensions are all aspects that help to impact your efficiencies. You should also look at the corrugations per inch.

Biomass

Hemp biomass is largely considered the non-food plant matter, or the non-reproductive parts of the plant. This includes the plant stalk, fibre and post-extraction matter, and excludes the plant flower and seeds (*Cannabis Tech*, 2018). Hemp biomass has many applications that will be discussed below. In order to harvest and make use of biomass, it either needs to be *dried*, or go through a process known as *retting*. Drying typically must be done in the time span of less than 1 week, while retting is a process that can take between 1-4 weeks. Drying a hemp plant is similar to drying of tobacco plants. Retting is a process that can be performed either wet or dry, and involves exposing the plant matter to moving water or to microorganisms that help breakdown the fibre of the plant. After retting, the processed material needs to be dried to prevent mold, rot or other forms of decay from affecting the biomass.

Biofuel

Hemp and Cannabis plant matter can also be converted into biofuels like biodiesel. There are actually two types of biofuels that can be produced from the hemp plant. First is biodiesel which is made from the oil of the pressed hemp seed. Biodiesel is considered a drop-in biofuel, which means that it already works with existing diesel engines. Railroad engines as well as commercial airlines have already demonstrated that biofuels can serve as industrial level solutions. Second is ethanol made from fermenting the stalk of the plant.

From a public policy perspective, biodiesel has already been encouraged as a substitute for fossil fuels. Biodiesel is currently the only alternative fuel to satisfy the EPA Tier I Health Effects Testing under section 211(b) of the Clean Air Act (Tyner, 2007). It has also been approved by several US government agencies as a low cost alternative fuel option for transportation fleets, under the Energy Policy Act (Birur et al., 2009).

Geography

Since the hemp plant is so versatile and resilient and requires less resources to grow in unstable environmental conditions, it is a strong candidate for filling industrialized needs in the least advantaged geographies on earth. Economically developing regions of the world as well as those that are geographically challenged can benefit from the sustainable use of the hemp plant.

Clothing

Fiber from the plant's stalk is strong, and until the development of synthetic fibers in the 1950s, it was a premier product used worldwide in making rope and clothing.

Medicine

The hemp plant is known to have many medicinal benefits and byproducts. "The top conditions being treated included anxiety (67%), insomnia (60%), joint pain and inflammation (52%) and depression (43%)" (Hildebrand, 2018). We will dive more into the medicinal benefits of the pant in Part 4.

Zoning of Hemp Cultivation, Repurposed Spaces and Past Legal Issues

Environmental sustainability can be just as much about using what already exists, and avoiding creating more of what is not necessary. With cities better understanding the opportunities to reactivate real-estate, abandoned buildings and underused zones, laws prohibiting the cultivation of hemp have been rolled back in recent years.

Logistics and Transportation

Cannabis is still considered federally in the United States a Schedule 1 substance, it cannot be directly transported over state lines. However, hemp, with a THC concentration of less than 0.3%, does have the opportunity to pass across state lines. This fact combined with existing agricultural infrastructure gives hemp an opportunity to establish the logistical supply chains that will eventually be utilized by cannabis products.

What are the Different Types of Extraction?

There are many different types of extraction methodologies. Let's begin with *lipid extraction* systems. THC and CBD are fat soluble (or lipid soluble), which means they dissolve in fats. We use olive oil or coconut oil to extract the compounds from the plant. The result is that it enhances the entourage effect mentioned earlier in the book, which is that qualities from terpene profiles are maintained post-extraction.

Lipid Extraction

Through lipid extraction you're not able to isolate certain chemical compounds in the same way that an *ethanol* or CO_2 *extraction* systems can. However, you are able to preserve a lot more of the terpenes. You have the ability to process about nine pounds of dry hemp plant every two hours. It achieves the standardized goal of about 99% CBD in the plant extraction process, and can be used with any kind of oil (including MCT, olive, almond, cherry seed, etc).

Low Solvent Methodology

Another extraction methodology is the *low solvent methodology*, where you use *PLC purification* systems with *CPC columns* to isolate the active compounds through natural product extracts. This is no different than the classic method of taking your hands and rubbing the hash against your hand to accumulate it as it sticks. It's a mechanical process, and it helps to maintain the purity of the compound. CPC stands for *centrifugal partition chromatography*. It is a cost effective alternative to common purification techniques (such as flash and prep HPLC) that yields a high quality of pure compounds. Using the CPC column, instead of flash and prep HPLC, means that we can use five times less solvent consumption. Typically, the processing amount is between 100 grams and about 10 kilos. You need to know the speed of the machines that do this processing (which are between 20 and 60 oscillations per minute) and the filter floor (which at regular level is about 400 microns to allow the kief to pass through.

Filters

Filters and filter bags for the machines that run CPC come in various sizes. On the low end they are 25 microns all the way up to 220 microns. This is important in measuring the amount of kief and process efficiency that is being passed through, in order to minimize the amount of waste. Typically, mechanical methods use a *pressure pneumatic* that is anywhere between about 500 pounds of pressure all the way up to eight tons (produced by a pneumatic lever that pulverizes and extracts the remaining material).

Dryers

When measuring dryers (either for home, business, or freeze dryers), you'll want to *measure the productivity in terms of gallons per day* in a batch processed. This can be as little as one or up to four gallons per 24-hour period. If you're looking at a scientific freeze-dryer (something more precise), you want to look at how many pounds per year can be utilized, or how many pounds per batch. This can be as low as 7 pounds per batch, or up to 16 pounds per batch.

When looking at drying systems, you also want to consider looking at drying trays and understanding what the shelf space and dimensions are. The primary metric to understand here is the *surface area* that is created by a three dimensional model. With some reasonable mathematical assumptions, you should be able to model and produce the entire cultivation cycle of the process.

Biomass Separation

Biomass separation and biomass centrifuges have two different metrics. We evaluate in biomass the *volumetric capacity*, which is *measured in square feet or in liters*. The *filtered surface area is measured in square feet*. Also important are the maximum G-forces from the centrifuges spinning speed, which typically range between 800 RPM and 1000 RPM in the separation process (Berthold et al., 1994). The basket RPM is also important to note, which could be between 1000 RPM and 2000 RPM. The *link suspension* is also very helpful in understanding how much is able to be processed of biomass at once (Google Patents, n.d.).

Biomass is a critical element in the process, because historically it's known to be used in many different industries as previously discussed, which is critical for our aggregate sustainability issues in the future. Biomass and biofuels are a potential lever against climate change ("Climate Change", 1990). The centrifuges used for biomass, and used for sustainable materials are able to process a basket RPM between 1000 and 2000. You want to know the *volumetric capacity either in cubic feet or in liters*. The filter surface area is in square feet.

An ideal biomass filtration system will minimize the amount of cost in time, equipment and opportunity to functionally minimize the dry spent fibers completely. You want to make sure that it's a *closed system* (meaning that there is no leakage, vapors, liquids or other risk of exposure). What makes investing in the right biomass drying system important is that they actually reduce your disposal costs by almost 100%. This is a major opportunity within the agri-system of designing a hemp or cannabis facility. It is important that the biomass drying system is low maintenance and that it is able to move its set temperature quickly and efficiently up and down. This enables it to turn on/off quickly.

Alcohol Extraction

Another type of extraction system is the *alcohol extraction* system. In addition to alcohol, this process may also utilize a propylene glycol water mixture. If you're operating at temperatures less than 7 degrees Celsius on a recirculating chiller, and you're trying to recover the solvent, you need to consider what is the *stream or flow* (let's say, 300 pounds per hour, the 60 CFM of air at 85 psi). You also want to make sure the filtering rate works quickly, where you can process up to 20 to 40 gallons per minute. The cost of the solvent must also be considered, with solvent costs ranging from less than $10 a gallon for alcohol to as high as $45 per gallon.

Butane Extraction

Butane extraction enables a large amount of product to be processed at a time but requires cold temperatures. Factors to consider in this process include a large maximum batch capacity (which is typically about 20-150 pounds), safety measures in place (like pressure shutdown, hydrocarbon leak shutdowns, solvent level and breathings). Butane extraction (which initiates at negative 85 degrees) presents a high explosion risk. For this reason, you want to make sure that it is hands-off and automated (Chan et al., 2017).

Ethanol Extraction

Ethanol extraction is another cold extraction method that initiates at a temperature of about negative 70 Celsius (it can be from negative 50 Celsius to negative 80 Celsius) (Romano & Hazecamp, 2013). Elements that impact the efficiency of an ethanol extraction system include material, low capacity, external collection tanks, extraction vessels, collection vessel volumes, and extraction vessel filters (the standard for these filters is about 40 microns). Safely working with ethanol, requires that the system use negative pressure to avoid risk of leaks or explosion. From a public policy and health and safety perspective, ethanol is the only solvent with the FDA Class III rating, meaning it is okay for exposure to humans. It can even be consumed (Romano and Hazecamp, 2013). Additionally, this form of extraction requires less infrastructure since ethanol does not need a C1D1 regulated room.

The most efficient way to use ethanol is to manipulate its polarity, so that it attaches itself to the cannabinoids and terpenes with pinpoint accuracy. Polarizing is helpful, because cannabinoids naturally dissolve in lipids, making it harder to dissolve in ethanol. An ultimate advantage of ethanol is that

Nima Veiseh

chlorophyll, fats, and waxes, which typically result in a less clear extract, are ignored during this ethanol extraction process. This means that you don't have to spend time, money, or resources on post-processing and purification.

Ethanol is one of the oldest and most proven means of extracting essential oils. The efficiency rate in this closed loop system is 98%. Different types of products can be extracted with this system (shatter, edibles, life resin, distillate, isolate, or a full reduction for vape pens). Purification is measured by the *ratio of THC to minor cannabinoid yield*. Because the extract is winterized, de-waxed, and free of chlorophyll, you'll also save valuable time and cost. The advantage of ethanol is that it deals with high volume efficiently.

Winterization and CO_2 Extraction

In an ethanol extraction process, *Winterization* is not required when there is inline filtration. For winterization with CO_2 extraction, what happens is the CO_2 extraction creates conditions where you can target certain molecules. Through CO_2 extraction process, above pressures and temperatures below the critical point, CO_2 becomes a *supercritical fluid* (Da Porto et al., 2012). Once the CO_2 is a supercritical fluid, it moves through the product and pulls out the active ingredients. The CO_2 is actually removed by temperature controlled expansion to atmospheric conditions. So all that remains is oil, without any residual solvents. The process for extraction to purification happens in five steps:

1)   Grinding the flour into fine particle sizes between a mesh that's between 40 and 600 microns. This is on the same order as fine coffee grounds.
2)   The ground up flour is loaded into the extraction machines that CO_2 passes through at the set temperature and pressure for extraction service to proceed.
3)   The acid group is removed through heating, leav-

ing only the neutral form of the cannabinoids in the oil (this is where TCHA, must be decarboxylated, in order to be converted into its active ingredient version of THC (this is the same process as going from CBDA to CBD).
4)   Purification (or *remediation*) takes place, where the cannabinoids are isolated and undesirable material (like pesticides, fungicides, etc) can be removed.
5)   Here we have the final product, that has been successfully extracted through *supercritical* CO_2 *extraction processing*.

Supercritical CO_2 purification can be as high as 95% (not as high as 98% or 99%) and it is solventless (Perrotin-Brunel et al., 2010). However, CO_2 extraction is relatively expensive compared to the other processes. When working with CO_2, you should look at a capacity, vessel size, flow rate, and pressure. These are all critical components. CO_2 also comes in three different types of scale series:

- Liquid-manual for small boutique construction.
- Hybrid-automated, which allows you to do true liquid and supercritical extractions.
- Liquid-automated, which utilizes CO_2 liquid and high flow rates to achieve the highest throughput in its class.

Liquid CO_2 chilling is required for passive recovery and de-waxing at negative 60 degrees Celsius. Another certain form of recovery is the *falling film evaporator*, where ethanol recovery is 150 liters per hour to 200 liters per hour. As far as the process for extraction, it can mostly can be distilled in seven stages through material handling, which involves the hammer mills that we discussed, conveyors and loaders. After that, there are the mixing tanks (which mix the raw material with a solvent and can be from 40 gallons up to 5,000 gallons per tank), and *filter presses* (which then filter the solvent). Storage tanks, which can be similar in scale to the mixing tanks are either jacketed or unjacketed. From there, winterization and *filtering* begins (this can be managed through filters, carbon filters, or lenticular cartridge filters). *Chillers* are used to get down to temperatures of negative 180 degrees Celsius.

With *falling film*, you can get a high throughput after solvent recovery. When doing falling film recovery, you want to control the input volume of ethanol based extract. This will tell you what the recovery is. If you have 300 gallons per hour, it is a good rate. Concentrated volume is about 20% of that. So you've got about an 80% recovery on the process. So you get 60 gallons per hour concentrated volume for every 300 gallons of extract in ethanol. You can operate it as either continuous or batch, which is a good binary variable. The evaporation temperature is important (which is about 30 degrees Celsius), but also using negative pressure is important (vacuums, as well as 70 TORR). Looking at the condenser cooling is also important, in order to complete the process of raw extraction or distillate extraction

A product that is a raw extract may still need to be distilled into an oil *isolate*. This is also critical for industries that require CBD concentrations to be high and THC to be low, because THC is still considered a Schedule 1 psychoactive substance.

Now that you've extracted the oils through different processes, how do you fill the machine and then test it? Well, there's different filling protocols and delivery methods to the consumer. There are several different methods, which could include cartridges, pods, darts, syringes, jars and capsules (these are the primary vessels). You want to make sure to minimize downtime and product loss in these cases, and look at different requirements as far as what needs to be done. This can either be *automated* or *fully automated* (an important binary variable when modeling your packaging system's efficiencies. The vessel's reservoir size of the oil is the key metric here and is typically measured in mLs.

Exploring the different ways to package the finished product will require that you can adjust volumes. If it's 140 milliliter container, you don't want to be off by more than one milliliter per stroke. There are also packaging alternatives that are available, such as pills and tablets. Tableting can be performed at a rate of 3,000 per hour. Pills can be up to 40,000.

Quality Assurance Testing

Remember, if you want to test what you've created, you typically want to do CPC (which is centrifugal partitioning chromatography, also known as counter current chromatography, or CCC). It's a preparative pilot industrial scale liquid purification technique that does not require traditional solid supports.

The main aim of this technology is to isolate the maximum amount of specific molecule at the highest purity in the minimum time. You do so without using any silica calm or supportive media. CBC and prep HPLC do have some similarities. They have a fundamental chromatographic process, and they're both trying to distill. They have very similar peripherals. They both have pumps, injectors, inline detectors, and faction plague tiles. The heart of the liquid chromatography system is the column where the separation occurs. The fundamental difference between LC (like flash, HPLC, and CBC), is the nature of the stationary phase. The stationary phase in classical liquid chromatography is made of a coated or non-coated silica. Skeleton particles are only supportive and the surface tends to generate interactions in the mobile phase while the compounds are being separated. CBC does not require solid support like silica.

The Sale

"A greater competitive market will drive prices down, as we've already seen on the west coast, where the plant has already been legalized for years."

Wholesale Market/Wholesale Price Positioning

Where does the oil go after it has been isolated and sold from the manufacturer? The oil is sold through wholesalers act as market makers for connecting producers with retailers. Wholesalers are under as much regulatory scrutiny as cultivators, and require special licenses to handle, sell and ship products.

The market position of the wholesaler means that is subject to important sensitivities in the market. Whether you are a cultivator, wholesaler or retailer, you are subject to market price changes from both your inputs and your outputs. The cultivators must be sensitive to the price of plant inputs that help grow their product (price taking), while at the same time being aware of the wholesale price in the market (price making). Retailers need to be sensitive to the wholesale price (price making) and at the same time the average retail selling price of that product (price taking). Wholesalers need to be able to work with cultivators to see what price they are willing to sell at (price maker) and, at the same time, need to be able to work with dispensaries to see what price they are willing to buy at (price maker).

Cultivators and dispensaries are in similar price positions because they each have at least 1 instance where they are forced to adhere to a commoditized, or largely non-negotiable, price. Cultivators cannot negotiate directly to drive down the price of watering their plants and, similarly, dispensaries are not actively negotiating with its customers to figure out what price to sell the product at, acting as price takers in each case. Wholesalers however are price makers in both cases: they negotiate actively with cultivators to decide on a price to buy raw goods, and they negotiate actively with dispensaries to decide on a price to provide final products. In both cases,

A greater competitive market will drive prices down, as we've already seen on the west coast, where the plant has already been legalized for years.

Interstate Commerce and Multi-State Operators (MSOs)

Companies need to uniquely structure as conglomerates that operate independently within states, but can be owned by a national investment vehicle. This business structure will change the moment that the "Federal Question" is answered.

Packaging: *What's the Complete Role of Packaging?*

Packaging is critical for a few reasons:

1) Regulatory reasons
2) The preservation of a product that is consumed
3) The integrity of that product

Packaging is also a core cost. By preserving the product and by sealing it, you preserve the value of the product in its weight. Thus, you want to make sure that humidity is maintained, since it makes up a measurable proportion of the products mass. Typically the levels of humidity is between 32% and 84% (with the most common being 62% to 58%). To properly regulate humidity, it's important to note that products, like Boveda, can be used to package items and preserve not just their state, but their value. You need less and less different types of humidity control elements, the larger your product size is, because as surface area increases the efficacy of your product to have controlled humidity through these products also increases as well. Why is relative humidity important in this case? Well, by maintaining the humidity in the right space, you can have up to 15% higher terpene content in the trichomes' retention.

Additionally, the reverse osmosis membrane allows for the water vapor to be clean and pure as it is emitted and regulated both ways through the package. This helps to inhibit mold. When you hold the relative humidity to less than 85% (this is the point where mold starts to grow), you can simplify the curing because of the two-way humidity controls to ensure you can keep everything at its optimum moisture. This may allow a team to maximize profits. Remember, you can lose up to 10% of the weight of the product during evaporation. Maintaining humidity also helps to maintain your value. You could lose up to 10% in transport to retail.

From a policy standpoint, it's also important that these packages (since they are controlled substances), meet certain US Code federalizations, like CFR 16 Part 1700.2, and also ASTM-D 3475. Childproofing is also a great necessity and responsibility. Certain patented technologies have created double flaps, and other ways to transport the product in a sealed container without allowing access to children (Anderson et al., 2019). Packaging is just as important for branding. My recent economic analysis has uncovered some interesting results around this:

In my recent economic analysis, we discovered that people are influenced by the differentiation between Indica and Sativa. People display a bias against hybrids and tend to seek out the purest strains. The names of the strains were also critical. This was shown in the study by reviewing 2,832 strains on Leafly with over 120,000 reviews. We tried to understand what the function of the experience was and what levers were affecting consumer decisions. We found the names of different cannabis strains tend to serve as levers and identifiers. For example, you'll find that Sativas tend to have the name Haze, while Indicas tend to have the name Kush (these are referred to as chemotaxonomic markers (Elzinga et al., 2015).

Retail Product and Delivery

The product can come in many different types of forms. To be noted as of now, the typical standard set of products includes gummies, chocolates, tinctures, vape cartridges, vape pens, vape kits, flour, pre-rolled joints, hempettes, creams, lotions, patches, roll-on gels, bath bombs, infused water, pet tinctures, pet treats (to name a few). Typically, products have an infusion of an isolate at 99% purity. If you're looking at something full spectrum, it's about 55% CBD oil (which means that it has less than a .3% THC, or THC free content). It should be *non-crystallizing* (this is a good binary variable), and has a broad terpene profile. It should be in a solution on its own and should not require any mixing or heating at room temperature. There have been recent advancements in technology for water soluble forms, since the FDA does not encourage the combustion of products. Vaping and ceramic technologies have become very popular, but states are beginning to ban them because of recent health implications. For the various delivery mechanisms offered in the industry, a key component is the body's ability to absorb. CBD tinctures and oil products may deliver as low as 100 milligrams, up to 2500 milligrams. Lexaria Bioscience has developed a turbo CBD absorption mechanism that results in faster absorption levels (measured in plasma concentration in micrograms per milliliter). This enables a faster onset/offset with a higher peak concentration level for consumers. Typically, starting to set in after about 30 minutes, then peaking within two hours. After peaking, it switches rates to a half life.

Machine Learning

In retail and throughout the industry, there is a growing opportunity for the integration of machine learning. For example, you can create an application that looks at the leaf while it's growing and it can tell you what disease the plant might have prior to harvesting. Usually, for vaporizing, you have a ceramic technology that heats up the temperature of the leaf to just below Fahrenheit 451, which enables this to vaporize the active ingredients (cannabinoids and terpenes), without affecting the product (Abrams, 2007).

What is Likely to Happen Involving Blockchain Technology?

Another important note in this product is to look at blockchain technology, and to understand how blockchain is going to affect the cannabis industry (Abelseth, 2018).

As mentioned earlier in this book, until an industry reaches maturity and institutions can help maintain them, major concerns are trust and accountability. Blockchain technology is one way of decentralizing trust and accountability, so we don't require an institution to act as a trust broker, or to hold transacting parties accountable. Blockchain uses public key encryption technology, similar to the technology used to protect your credit card when you make purchases online, in order to create a transaction record that cannot be modified once it is entered. Blockchain is a cryptographic prime number factorization backed database, where a ledger cannot be altered without you leaving your unique mark on it. In order to prevent fraudulent records from being wrongly verified, blockchain technology uses a method of *distributed consensus*, where people previously on the record can anonymously verify whether that record is accurate. Bitcoin is one of the most famous examples of Blockchain technology. Since every Bitcoin can be tracked from person to person, every time it changes hands, this means you can trust the coin that you've been given is a real coin, which you can also verify. This is no different than how government currency works -- if you look at any bill, there are not only a myriad of features on the bill to prevent it from being counterfeited, but every major currency note in the world contains a unique serial number that is registered to the treasury that issued it.

Blockchain technology can also be used to track physical goods, just like financial assets. In the Cannabis industry, Blockchain technology allows customers in the industry to securely and transparently trace the entire supply chain from harvest to product distribution (Crosby et al., 2016). The customer can enter the order's information, or scan a QR code, and you instantly gain access to certificates of analysis, safety data sheets, harvest information, and other critical data. Blockchain ensures no information gets lost or altered and guarantees that the customers receive the genuine, high quality experience they deserve.

Three-Tier System

"The two means of controlling the alcohol industry were by: taxation and dividing it into 3 tiers, producers, distributors and retailers."

When a new market opens with no precedent, it is not uncommon to try and find the closest comparable. In this case, the sudden legitimization of the cannabis industry finds its closest analogy in the repeal of the prohibition of alcohol in 1933. The *three-tier system* that emerged was meant to control the alcohol industry using two mechanisms so states could feel in control of an industry that had been stigmatized over the "roaring 1920s". The two means of controlling the alcohol industry were by: taxation and dividing it into 3 tiers, producers, distributors and retailers. The three tiers meant that people could be prevented from vertically integrating the alcohol industry, by not allowing companies to hold licenses in all 3 tiers.

When analyzing how a three-tier system might affect a market, you analysis should look at least two variables that will drive the analysis. First is the *supply of licenses by tier* at each tier. According to the laws of supply and demand, the lower the number of licenses, the lower the manufacturing capability of the market and the lower the supply, making demand more difficult to meet leading toward higher prices. Second is the *taxation level by tier*. The higher the taxes, the higher the prices. The taxation level can be seen as a *political cost* that gets passed to the consumer. This in turn may imply lower demand from consumers, and lower demand for entrants to the market to get licenses (Duffy, 2009).

Cannabis Licenses and Market Segments

In order to participate in the market for cannabis, every country that has a non-illicit market for cannabis has a legal and regulatory framework to manage the stakeholders and market entrants. One of the most important economics characteristics of the cannabis market at this point in history, is that there are no incumbents. It is a market where everyone is an entrant, which is impossible unless the market was being legitimized for the first time. This assumption is an important consideration when modeling how these markets will grow and organize.

As of the publication of this edition, only two countries in the world have full legalized cannabis, Canada and Uruguay. It is important to measure *global market penetration* because as market penetration grows, borders connect, transportation costs decrease and more opportunities for commerce occur, we are likely to see an exponential expansion in the market for cannabis (Krugman, 1991). Thus, as of the publication of this book, the global market penetration is 1.03%, which is calculated by the number of countries fully legalizing divided by the total number of member countries in the United Nations (193). The use of the United Nations as the basis of the total country count is justified because the United Nations is the largest governing body that deals with the regulation of cannabis. These major treaties include: The Single Convention on Narcotic Drugs from

1961, the Convention on Psychotropic Substances in 1971, and the Convention against Illicit Traffic in Narcotic Drugs and Psychotropic Substances in 1988.

When performing an economic analysis of different business segments it is best to divide business by their legal standing. This is helpful for two reasons. First, this method divides business by their size. Know how large a business means you know how much impact it might have on the surrounding market and the types of assumptions you need to make about it when performing an analysis. For example, the economic and market assumptions for a large grow house will be different than a small grow house. According to industrial organization theory, a large grow house is more likely to be a *price maker* in the market, while a small grow house is likely to be a *price taker*. This means that large grow houses are going to have a larger impact on the overall competitive market price for what cannabis is sold at and can have more market power in purchasing supplies and negotiating with wholesalers. Conversely, modeling a small grow house means that they take the price from the market as input, and need to be aware of how they are being affected.

The second way that license type helps us to better organize business segments is that they are also divided by how they create their product. By looking at the license type, you can see whether the product produced from that grower was grown indoor or outdoors, which might have a profound impact on the types of infrastructure investments the company made as well as the amounts of inputs that needed to go into the growing process. License type as a categorical variable will allow you to analyze the quality of a product from the consumer perspective at a deeper level.

License Type is an example of a *categorical variable* that is useful to have in your models, because it will allow you to separate the effects that different market players may have in your models.

Below is a set of 17 standard license types that can be used ("State License", 2019).

Type 1 is for Boutique Cultivation Activity, or small farmers. This license can be distributed to the state, and typically requires no major federal oversight. Small farming activity may be up to 5,000 square feet of total canopy size or up to 50 plants. For reference in understanding the scale of these operations, a American Football field is 57,600 square feet. Type 1 licences can be divided into three sublicenses, A, B or C, which are for outdoor, indoor or *mixed-light growers*, respectively. Mixed Light growers are those that may use artificial light to supplement natural light from the outdoors.

Type 2 is for Small Cultivation Activity. This license can be distributed to the state, and typically requires no major federal oversight. Medium farming activity may be from 5,001 to 10,000 square feet of total canopy size. Similarly to above, Type 2 licences can be divided into three sublicenses, A, B or C, which are for outdoor, indoor or mixed-light growers, respectively.

Type 3 is for Medium Cultivation Activity. This license affects such large growers that the Department of Food and Agriculture will typically regulate and mandate these licenses. For Sublicense A in this category, or outdoor growing, you can grow from 10,001 square feet up to 43,560 square feet (1 acre). For Sublicense B in this category, or indoor growing, you grow a total canopy size of 10,001 to 22,000 square feet (0.5 acre). For Sublicense C or mixed light growing, you can grow a total canopy size of 10,001 to 22,000 square feet (0.5 acre) as well.

Type 4 is for Large Cultivation Activity. It has the same structure as the Type 3 licenses, as well as the A, B and C subcategories, however, each of the canopy sizes are greater than 22,000 square feet.

Type 5 is a license for a nursery. A nursery is a place where plans are grown into their vegitative states, however, they cannot produce any flowers or buds. They usually cultivate seeds or make clones of the mother plant that they will then sell, assisting their plants "on photosynthesis and accumulating resources needed for flowering and reproduction" ("Cannabis Nursery Ordinance", 2017).

License Types 6 and 7 both deal with the post processing of the plant and manufacturing of oils and distillates. Both of these licences are regulated at the state level. The difference between them is that Type 6 Manufacturers deal with non-volatile solvents, like CO_2, water, dry ice, cooking oils or ethanol. Type 7 Manufacturer deal with volatile solvents like butane, propane and hexane.

License Type 8 is for Testing facilities. This is to license companies to provide Certificates of Analysis that show the contents of the product, and give the chemical breakdown of what is inside each crop. What makes this license unique is that if you have a License Type 8, you are not allowed to have any other type of license. This makes sense for accountability and information asymmetry issue, because there is a potential conflict of interest if a company is allowed to both produce a product and test it.

License Type 9 and Type 10 are for Retailers. Both need to have a registered premise for sale, however Type 9 means your a retailer that does not have a public storefront, while Type 10 means that you do have a public storefront. Each Type also has two sublicense types A or M, for Adult-use or Medicinal-use, respectively. Depending on the local laws, the number of dispensaries owned under a license can be limited to as few as three.

Type 11 is for Distribution or Wholesellers. They are responsible for distributing and transporting the product between cultivators, manufacturers, dispensaries, and/or testing facilities. They are also usually expected to have License Type 12, which is for Transportation. Also as a matter of preventing conflicts of interest, Type 11 holders are not allowed to have a license in cultivation, manufacturing or dispensing.

The Canadian-American Border and Instrumental Variable Analysis

"Since it is not legal to trade across borders, data does not exist to let us directly measure that. However that does not mean that product is not moving across the border. So what do you do in economics when you have a hard time measuring something directly?"

With few countries with legalized cannabis markets, we are not able to see the effects of the movement of cannabis across borders. However, this analysis has important public policy, drug trafficking and economic implications. If product can move across borders, that means that pricing of products needs to include variables in two different countries.

An important factor to measure is the activity across the Canadian-American Border. Since it is not legal to trade across borders, data does not exist to let us directly measure that. However that does not mean that product is not moving across the border. So what do you do in economics when you have a hard time measuring something directly? You use an *instrumental variable* (Angrist et al, 1996). An instrumental variable is a variable that is correlated to the variable we are trying to measure, while we make some key assumptions. For example, while we cannot directly measure the amount of cannabis moving across the border, we can use "number of cannabis traffic violations at US-Canada border" as an instrumental variable. If we make the assumption that the number amount of cannabis moving across the border is linear and proportional to the amount of cannabis being produced, we are able to estimate how much product is being trafficked across the border. This analysis may reveal to policy makers that legalization will not only save in law enforcement costs but also increase tax revenue, both of which are compelling factors in legalizing cannabis at the Federal level.

Banking and the Evolution of Trust

*"The one factor to consider when measuring the velocity of money, that may negatively impact a market is **leverage**."*

The foundation of every business transaction is in trust, and creating institutions to grow and protect trust is critical in a new market. On Sept 24th, 2019, the US House of Representatives passed the Secure And Fair Enforcement (SAFE) Banking Act. The law allowed banks and credit unions to process transactions and store assets for companies that engage in cannabis business. Companies could worry less about managing cash business, which can be subject to theft or not reported for taxation. Businesses can also transact with each other more fluidly, increasing the *velocity of money* in the market. The velocity of money is an important economic growth factor when performing a market analysis, and represents the number of times a dollar is transacted within an industry over an interval of time. It is a major indicator of the health of a market, because people doing more business is always better for business. The one factor to consider when measuring the velocity of money, that may negatively impact a market is *leverage*. Leverage is when companies borrow money in order to execute their transactions and may distort the amount of value that is actually being created. The Great Recession of 2008 and the subprime loan crisis is a good example of the problems that can occur if leverage is not correctly monitored and accounted for.

Delivery Systems Post Processing for Retail Consumption

"What does it mean to be a cannabis plant?"

Flower

One flower, Many Terms

Traditionally, you might have heard names like "ganja", "weed" or "marijuana" used to describe cannabis. These alternative names have contributed to some of the confusion and lingering stigmas that historically surround the plant. Various names have been adopted and altered across generations.

The word "ganja", for example, has been mistakenly tied to Rastafarian religion, while the true root of the name comes from Hindi (adopted into common use, as a result of the British using Indian labor circa 1845 on plantations in Jamaica). Ganja, in Hindi, refers to the buds on the flower. The word "marijuana" is a reinterpretation of the Spanish term *marhijuana,* used to describe the cannabis sativa plant. Weed, alternatively, crept into the english language during the 90's and offered a substitute for "grass", used by our "hippie" generation from the 60's. The earliest uses of the Latin name *cannabis,* comes from Carl Linnaeus in 1753.

What does it mean to be a cannabis plant? They can be recognized as male, female or even hermaphroditic. This process of identification happens during the pre-flowering stage (after the vegetative stage and before the flowering stage). They are best known for their iconic fan-like leaves, stretching from skinny stems with budding cola. Nodes on the plant are where hormones are produced and most growth takes place. Female plants are producers of resin and are harvested for their rich THC content for consumption (Rahn, 2019). These are preferred by most growers. Male plants are shorter in stature, with visible sacks that get filled with pollen. They characteristically contain a higher concentration of cannabinoids and terpenes, in comparison to female plants. We rely on these male plants for hemp products and textiles that are rapidly surfacing in our retail environment.

How Does the FDA Regulate Cannabis?

Both male and female plants are incredibly useful to us, although female plants are still experiencing stricter federal regulations. In 2019, the federal government regulates all drugs through the Controlled Substance Act (CSA). They treat female cannabis like a highly addictive and deadly, controlled substance. They have not yet fully recognized that these plants have medicinal value (Benowitza and Henningfield, 2018).

Recently, the Agriculture Improvement Act of 2018 (Farm Bill) eliminated cannabis products low in THC (<.03%) from the Controlled Substance Act, although the FDA still retains responsibility and control over all cannabis-derived products that get introduced into the market. The FDA claims that there still remain questions to be answered surrounding the science, safety and quality of cannabis production, although they recognize that cannabis-derived products could have therapeutic opportunities. They simply rely on applicants and scientific investigators to conduct research and make sure that the final product meets statutory standards for approval. We are still in the early stages of navigating this regulatory relationship. The FDA has issued three *generally recognized as safe* (GRAS) notices for hemp-derived products. This includes hulled hemp seed (GRN765), hemp seed protein powder (GRN771) and hemp seed oil (GRN778). These noticies are what have enabled us to use hemp as a source of nutrients, in addition to beverages, soups, dips, spreads, baked goods, cereals, and snacks (CFSAN, 2018).

How do we measure the Flower?

Cannabis flower is measured in grams, ounces, pounds and kilograms for simplicity. One gram is a metric unit of mass equal to one-thousandth of a kilogram. This is a small unit for measurement, that has become familiar to consumers and prevalent on product packaging. An ounce is a larger measurement (28g) and can be broken down into eighths (3.5g), quarters (7g) or half ounce (14g). One pound consists of (448g) or is the same as 16 ounces. One kilogram is equivalent to 35.3 ounces. Kilograms are typically used by those in the industry (typically buyers or dispensary owners) who are dealing with mass quantities at wholesale prices (Smart et al., 2017).

Because cannabis flower is measured and priced by mass, it becomes a challenge when a batch of any size loses weight, therefore losing part of it's value. Transporting cannabis requires the active stabilization of environmental conditions, namely humidity. This is critical for reducing the onset of mold and retaining the freshness of the batch. Products like Boveda offer technology that allows for an automatic two-way management system, that can increase or decrease moisture in the air using natural ingredients ("Why Boveda is Different", n.d.).

Vape Technologies

There are two main types of vaping technologies: oven vapes and atomizers.

Oven vapes typically take flower as input and heat it to the temperature between 350 and 450 degrees fahrenheit. We might ask, what is so special about this temperature range? The special aspect of this temperature range is that you can heat the leaf without the cellulose in the leaf combusting. If you have ever read the book Fahrenheit 451 by Ray Bradbury, you will know that the book gets its name from the temperature at which the paper of books burn. Paper is made of cellulose from tree pulp, similar to a cannabis leaf. Thus if you heat the leaf to just above

350 degrees but below 450 degrees, the leaf is hot enough that the cannabinoids and terpenes vaporize into the air which you can inhale but the leaf does not burn and create smoke and tar.

Atomizers are another vaping technology typically used with oils. An atomizer contains a coil that heats up to a high enough temperature, usually between 400 and 450 degrees fahrenheit, and turns the oil into a vapor. The coil has a resistance that can be measured in ohms (usually about 1 ohm), and comes with a battery that powers the coil. The battery size is measured in units called *mAh, or milli amp hours*, with values typically in the range of 200 to 900mAh.

A Convergence of Technology Standards: 510, Ruby, Juul

Currently there are different sets of technological standards in the vape world, and how this market evolves will be interesting to watch. Currently there are 3 major companies for vape cartridges and it will be fascinating to see how they end up either working together, segmenting off into their own niches, or being put out of business. The 510 cartridge is not owned by any particular brand, and is named after the shape of the threads used to connect the cartridge to the battery, 10 threads spanning 5 mm in length. This is an open standard that any company can use and attaches to any 510 threaded battery.

On the other hand, Juul and Ruby are both vape cartridge standards made by private companies. Juul has the advantage of access to the nicotine market, while Ruby is taking the more boutique approach and courting cannabis dispensaries directly. Similarly, as of the writing of this book, there are few standards for batteries in the industry, which has led to batteries typically failing very quickly. Store owners interviewed for this book would frequently comment about how many batteries consumers would keep repurchasing due to the high failure rate reported by their customers. The result of this market evolution will likely be documented in future versions of this book.

From the perspective of a data scientist, it is important to keep track of how a product is delivered to a client. If you know the type of cartridge they use, you can also dive more deeply into the types of experiences consumers are having. For example, you may find that a store had a very sudden increase in vape cartridge sales, and then suddenly the sales dropped heavily. If you dive deep into the analysis, you may find that the store was offering 510 cartridges, which have a tendency to break when people put them in their pockets, do to the strain on the connector itself. Once consumers realize the 510 cartridges break, they may be less inclined to buy them in the future. By responsibly performing the analysis, you can create actionable insight which many mean adjusting the types of cartridges sold to account for the preferences of the consumer.

Health Impact and Event-Driven Analysis

As of October 2019, there have been 1,299 reported cases of lung injuries related to vaping including 26 deaths, according to the Center for Disease Control (CDC, 2019). The issue was with the use of Vitamin E Acetate used in the vaping oils, suspected of causing severe cough in those that ingested it (Sun, 2019). The news of the deaths and a federal crackdown on the distribution of vape cartridges marked one of the very first *exogenous events* to impact the cannabis industry. An *exogenous event* or *exogenous factor* is an event that comes from outside of the model, and can impact the market. It is not caused directly by the market, but rather is something that the market reacts to.

Event driven analysis is typically a type of *time series analysis*, where you perform the analysis along a timeline, and look at the effect that an event has on a market before and after it occurs. For example, many people expected that demand for cartridges and cannabis in general would drop, since the market was only newly regulated, raising fears that there could be contamination in other products. While some distributors reported a spike in the sale of flower over cartridges, it appears that the market as a whole has not been severely impacted by the health scare.

Another important case for event driven analysis, and the implications on public health, are regarding the question, why did it take 1,299 reported lung injuries and 26 deaths in order for their to be a policy intervention? The answer is in two more specific questions: 1) where was the data of these reports coming from? And 2) was there a standardized alert mechanism in place to monitor such reported events? The answer to the first question is that this data was largely dependent on the accurate reporting of those that suffered and those that treated them. If the deaths occurred in states during times when cannabis was illegal, it is likely that they did not report the truth about their vape use, thus preventing authorities from picking up the lead on this issue. Similar concerns have been raised in similar policy situations, for example, when the US Government tried to implement a citizenship question on the census. Advocacy groups argued successfully that this may discourage minorities and those with uncertain citizenship status to not report to the census for risk of being identified for a violation. It was decided that the importance of having an accurate census, through which congressional districts are mapped and resources are allocated, was of greater interest to the public good than including the question. Similarly, public health policy would benefit by collecting more data and staying ahead of these issues by identifying means of collecting data in a way that respondents are most likely to honestly disclose. Blockchain technology and tagging along the entire supply chain is one way of doing so.

Second, although reports of this issue may have been collected for many years, it was not until a critical threshold of deaths occurred that a public policy intervention took place. It appears that reports coming in as a normal distribution was not sufficient to trigger an alert. It appears to have taken a sudden uptick in the rate or concentration of deaths in a smaller period of time that raised suspicions, although it is not clear which metric was used and what that threshold was. Health policy in a world of big data requires planning and anticipation of how data can be used to protect the public interest.

Environmental Impact and The Bathtub Curve

How are all the cartridges and batteries being disposed? Not consistently. Until a federal mandate is put in place for such products. While there are currently laws that require that batteries be disposed of safe and non-hazardous ways, batteries are the cigarette butts of the 21st century, and creating strong incentives for proper disposal may be a priority for lawmakers to address (Chang, 2014). Taxes and deposits have been used with success in the past to promote proper disposal of these products, similar to the ten cent deposit that the State of Michigan levies on recyclable items, but this is just one of several possible incentive mechanisms.

An important model for data science we borrow from engineering is the idea of a bathtub curve graph, named for the shape that it resembles. A bathtub curve graph is meant to predict the failure rates of devices, and understanding when and how a device fails can help to prevent future device failures, help to raise consumer confidence, and lower the amount of environmental waste. A bathtub curve has time on the x-axis (independent variable) and the number of devices that failed at that point in time on the y-axis (dependent variable). We call the independent and dependent variables because the number of devices failed depends on the point of time we are at. The curve starts high at time zero, drops low as the device ages, and then rises again later in the time series. The stylized fact in engineering is that devices are most likely to fail at the beginning of their life, when they are fresh off the assembly line and untested, and at the end of their lives, when they have been worn down over a long period of use. By performing *anomaly detection analysis* against this pattern, we may find opportunities to reduce the average rate at which devices fail.

Analysis of Product Content and What Reaches the Consumers' Hands

"There's been much debate, since there is no regulated or standardized way of performing a C of A. We continue to debate about what it should contain. Regardless, the C of A will be a long-standing procedure in understanding what goes into the plants. It is important for you as a stakeholder, executive, or data scientist to understand the units behind this as we go through it."

What Does Chemical Analysis Tell Us?

Expect that a THC dominant strain is going to have somewhere between 8% and 32% THC at the outer bounds, but typically it will be close to 12% to 27% THC per percentage of dry weight. If you're getting a CBD dominant strain, then the total CBD dry weight may be from 4% up to 24%. The highest concentration is typically a bounded level of CBD (expected in a CBD dominant strain) between 10% and 15%. The strains that are balanced in terms of their percentages, tend to have between 8% and 12% of both CBD and THC.

This can also be measured as the THC to CBD ratio. And in our case, we'd call this a 1:1. For THC heavy brands, the ratio would be 20:1, whereas it can similarly be 1:20 for CBD heavy brands. The THC to CBD ratio can also be 14x up to 80x, as we have seen the shift from 1995 to 201 (El Sohly and Church, 2016).

Analysis Methods

To understand the chemical composition within the plant, *gas chromatography* with a flame ionization detector method can be used. This basically means that the plant has been vaporized and there's been a *spectrographic analysis* of the different compounds within it. Next we will review a series of bounded analysis, so that you can understand the range and units of measure of the different compounds in THC and CBD. We will also explore the inactive, un-psychoactive ingredients, like the terpenes.

The important thing in gas chromatography analysis is that ultimately the process produces something in the industry that we call a C of A, or a *Certificate of Analysis*. There's been much debate, since there is no regulated or standardized way of performing a C of A. We continue to debate about what it should contain. Regardless, the C of A will be a long-standing procedure in understanding what goes into the plants. It is important for you as a stakeholder, executive, or data scientist to understand the units behind this as we go through it. This analysis was performed by examining 255 different strains. This is by no means a whole universe of data.

To give you an example, at the time of this analysis, there were 2,832 strains registered in the Leafly website. So this is a small sample, relatively speaking. According to others in the field, it is relatively comprehensive. The ratio of THC to CBD is the unit for what we call, *potency testing*. For *safety testing*, the elements that go into that analysis are mold, mildew, bacterial analysis with microbes, pesticide residue analysis, terpene analysis, flavonoid analysis, residual solvent analysis from extracts, and other heavy metal analysis.

Note: Recently it was discovered that lead was found in products, not because the plant grower in the United States used lead in the ingredients, but the equipment that they purchased from China and other countries did not have the proper certification, and some of those heavy metals leaked into their product.

Here are the units for testing in this case. When we refer to a percentage of THC, that means a 100 milligram sample of dried plant material is ground up and dissolved in 30 milliliters of solvent. If recreation cannabis has an expected concentration of 20% THC, then this means that for every hundred milligrams of dried plant material, we find 20 milligrams of THC dissolved in 30 milliliters of solution. That could also be interpreted as 667 micrograms per milliliter of concentrate. Typically, an analysis for gas chromatography takes roughly about 10 minutes, which will give you a better idea for how often, how quickly, something can be processed.

Since also understanding how long it takes for something to happen is a proxy for how many resources to deploy (either in employed human capital or physical capital), you will want to understand its effect on the total life cycle of the development and quality assurance testing (QA testing) of the product.

The procedure for creating a uniform sample for gas chromatography involves randomly taking a sample from the plant section of the leaf bud and the flower, if available. Then you dry the plant material for two hours at 385 degrees Celsius in a well ventilated environment. Following this, you weigh out approximately 100 milligrams of dried plant material and grind that sample to a powder to pass through a 1 millimeter sieve to filter it (1 millimeter is the standard for the ground flower). Next, you add 30 milliliters of organic solvent, and then you sonicate it (or shake it up for 30 minutes to make sure it fully dissolves). You then filter, which would give you the opportunity to convert THCA to THC (Dussy et al., 2004). Remember that THCA and CBDA cannot be detected by gas chromatography because the decarboxylation does require to observe THC. This means that the THCA is converted and no longer measurable in the plant. Evaporating the same to dryness at 200 degrees Celsius for 20 minutes occurs before reconstituting the organic solvent and then performing the analysis by gas chromatography.

With a short diameter column used to test the sample, the separation of the cannabinoids can happen in less than 3 minutes. The amount of time it takes for a 3 minute number comes from the amount of time it takes for a sample, based on a 1 millimeter grinding, to fully devolve into its cannabinoid components. Looking at a gas chromatography analysis, you're going to notice basically three peaks. The first peak represents the CBD and CBC peaks. The second set of peaks involve THC. And the third main peak involves CBN. If you see a graph that has a major peak on the left but no other peaks, it must be a high CBD cannabis, as discovered through the gas chromatography. If you see a strain with a middle peak but no other peaks, then it is likely high THC content.

Other elements that can be introduced in testing include a microscopic or qualitative analysis to look for color consistency, debris, stems, seeds, contaminants, and other adulterants. Adulterants can be natural or they can be added to plant materials. They can also be visually identifiable.

The THC and CBD potency is another analysis that can be performed. This method of THC or CBD ratio potency does not have a state by state guideline, but it rather there are DEA guidelines for this. The primary method the DEA uses is gas chromatography. And the reported unit is in percentage THC relative to the original plant material weight.

THC and Cannabinoid Profiles

So, before we dive into types of terpenes, let's look at the basic unit of measurement and the type of bounded analysis that we use to understand how total CBD and total THC is measured. The standard unit set for this is percentage dry weight. The bounded analysis for most THC dominant strains reveals that THC dominant strains have some predictable characteristics.

CBD to THC Ratios

The CBD:THC Ratio (or CTR) ius meant to reflect different physical and medical benefits to the consumer. The *CTR* can be represented as a ratio, e.g. 4:1, and reflects the proportion of CBD to THC in the product. A ratio of 1:1 means you're getting a higher THC to CBD ratio, which will result in more psychoactive effects. A ratio of 20:1 means that you're getting a higher CBD to THC ratio, and will feel little if any psychoactive effects (Wall et al., 2019). In fact, research says that CBD may actually counteract the psychoactive effects of THC.

1:0 means the product is nearly all CBD focused, while 0:1 means the product is nearly all THC focused. It is not common to see ratios published on products as either 1:0 or 0:1 because the CTR is meant to portray a spectrum of balance between CBD and THC. If you see these types of ratios arise in your data, you should consider creating a *pipeline filter* to catch potential anomalies in your data (*anomaly detection*), so you can give it a second look.

The ratios range within the interval of 1:1 for the most CBD light, up to 20:1 for the most CBD heavy. *Bounded analysis* can be helpful here when you want to measure the response of a consumer to a range of CBD products, by reducing the scope of the analysis to a range that looks specifically at CBD related effects, which might mean just looking at products that are between a ratio of 4:1 and 20:1. If you instead tried to include the whole range of products with ratios outside those bounds, you might have a harder time measuring the effects you're searching for as well as include customers in your analysis that you aren't meant to actually be targeting.

CBD, THC and Terpene Measurements

Now, let's profile the different terpenes. Terpenes are what give flavor to the cannabis plant, but have no psychoactive effects. Similar to how someone might say that a wine has certain notes of oak (or a flower), terpenes provide that similar effect. Terpenes are actually produced by many plants, not just cannabis. They are responsible for the flavor profiles and scent profiles of those different plants.

A-pinene

Alpha pinene (or A-pinene), is found in the oils of coniferous trees. It is also the most common terpene in cannabis (and in the plant world). It helps enhance breathing by being a bronchodilator, promotes alertness, and helps with memory retention. In our analysis, we found that the A-pinene profile is on average .90 with a min of 0, and a max of 5.61. A-pinene has that aroma of pine and it vaporizes at 411 degrees Fahrenheit (or 155 degrees Celsius). It is also found in pine needles, rosemary, basil, parsley, dill, and orange peels. It is the most fragrant and prevalent of oils secreted in cannabis trichomes, which is primarily the flower.

As a percentage of measured terpenes, A-pinene can typically be in the 20 to 30% range. It is more common in strains like AK47, Blue Dream, and responsible for the piney note that emerges from strains like Pineapple Express (hybrid strains, and more Indica leaning strains). It also has the scent of eucalyptus, since it is related to that plant. Another thing to note before we dive further into terpenes is the different ways to measure the THC to CBD scale. It can be measured as a percentage of dry weight, as well as milligrams, with a lower bound percentage of 2.5% (corresponding to 1 milligram) and the upper bound of 25% (corresponding to flower) and pre rolls of 25% (corresponding to 20 milligrams). In the case of the concentrate, the 25% matches to the 80% and that's in the bounded analysis, and also corresponds to 20 milligrams.

CB1 receptors are supposed to be receiving THC, which can

create effects of euphoria, relaxation, anxiety reduction, and short-term memory impairment. Alternatively, they can increase anxiety and impair your short term memory. That happens when THC bonds with the CB1 receptors. When CBD attaches to the CB1 receptor, it prevents THC from bonding and decreases the negative side effects of THC, which also decreases anxiety and short-term memory loss. This is why CBD is known to have anti-anxiety effects. CBD is also known to affect the same receptors that affect opioids, dopamine, and serotonin, through a direct interaction.

Myrcene

This terpene is found in cannabis, lemon grass, hops, and other plants. It's a pain reducer, antispasmodic, anti-inflammatory, and has other properties. Myrcene gives off an earthy, musty quality, and has citrus overtones. It can also be found in thyme, parsley, and cardamom. It is also an important component in the perfume industry because it has a nice smell to it, but is not used directly (typically it is used as a supplement). Myrcene can also be converted into Myrcenol, which is a fragrance found in lavender.

Myrcene is also measured as beta-myrcene, as a terpene that is found in these different elements. Its effects may also be sedative as well, in addition to being anti-inflammatory and antibiotic. Strains that have typically been known for their myrcene content are the White Widow, Jack Herer, Himalayan Gold, and Pink Cush, as well as Pure Cush. In my analysis of 225 strains, I find an average myrcene content of 4.28, with a max of 24.47. It has a standard deviation of 3.7.

Limonene

Limonene has a lemon odor and takes its name from the lemon itself. It has anti-anxiety, anti-depressant, antibiotic, and anti-oxidant properties and is quite often found in the peels of citrus fruits and other plants. Limonene has a citrus aroma, it vaporizes at 348 degrees Fahrenheit (or 176 degrees Celsius) and can be found in fruit rinds, rosemary, juniper, and peppermint. It has the medical value of reducing anxiety, depression, inflammation, pain, and cancer symptoms (in addition to stress, sleep, and elevating mood). Limonene or D-limonene as it is scientifically known, comes under analysis to an average of 2.12, with a max of 6.93, and a standard deviation of 1.5- This means that it's about 1 to 2% of dry weight.

Eucalyptol

Eucalyptol is a terpene that is also known as 1,8-cineole. It's a popular terpene that has a refreshing eucalyptus scent and can also be in tea tree as well. It's antifungal, anti-bacterial and anti-inflammatory. It helps especially in the digestive system and sinuses. In my analysis, we see that eucalyptol is very "trace", with a max of .13, an average of .007, and a standard deviation of .02.

Linalool

Next is linalool, which has an herbal, minty, cinnamon, and rosewood smell and odor to it. It's therapeutic effects are anti-anxiety, sedative, pain reduction, and anti-epileptic. Linalool in our analysis has an average of .78 among the strains, a max of 4.95, with a standard deviation of .84. Linalool is a terpene that is predominant in coriander and lavender. It has a floral aroma and is popular particularly in Cush strains, like Master Cush, Pink Cush, as well as Amnesia Haze.

Terpineol

Terpineol, has a sharp pine smell and is related to the lamiaceae family. Terpineol is a combination of four monoterpene alcohol isomers and it occurs in many plants, including cannabis. Up to 150 plants display this terpene. It has a high boiling point of about 424 degrees Fahrenheit. It occurs in pine trees and lilacs as well. It is an antibiotic, anti-oxidant, anti-tumor, sedative, anti-inflammatory, anti-malarial, and anti-xylitolic. It is common in Jack Herer, White Widow, Girl Scout Cookies and OG Cush. In our analysis, the terpene level for terpineol is about .90, with a high of 14.1.

Menthol

There is also menthol, which is a mint odor, and anti-inflammatory properties.

Citronellol

Citronellol is found in roses and geraniums and has a citronella smell.

Caryophyllene

Caryophyllene is the most common of the terpenes in cannabis hops and rosemary. It has an anti-inflammatory, antidepressant quality. It also has an anti-alcoholic affect and a smell that is spicy and earthy. According to our analysis the concentration is about 3.07. The standard distribution deviation of 2.18 means it's a very high range since the standard deviation is almost as great as the mean itself, which is important to recognize. The max is a 14.25.

Humulene

Humulene is the most common essential oil found in hops and also is found. Humulene has an evergreen, spicy odor and can help with anxiety, neurosis and inflammation effects.

Terpinene

Terpinene is also one of the cannabinoids we find in cardamom and margin oils. Terpinene can be found in its alpha form or in its Y form, both have similar effects and concentrations of about .02 to .03, with a concentration maximum of .6.

Pesticides

Pesticides and fungicides show up in the plant testing, since they're used in the plants. A common trend now is to use natural pesticides or non-chemical pesticides to prevent contamination of the final material with artificial chemicals. The individual states throughout our country do not have specific methods of regulation, however, procedures for pesticide and fungicidal guidelines and administration are mandated federally by the EPA (Bascietto et al. 1990). The testing procedure that is used for testing for pesticides and fungicides is called SPE or *Solid Phase Extraction*. The units used to measure pesticides is PPM or Parts Per Million. Most regulatory agencies require that a plant has no more than .1 PPM of any pesticide.

Pesticides, molds and other trace chemicals of the process

Terpenoids, or terpenes (the flavoring element responsible for the distinct smell of cannabis) can also be tested. Terpenes can be identified and tested through gas chromatography and mass spectrometry.

Pesticides can be classified as either *chlorinated hydrocarbons* or *carbonate pesticides*. You get chlorinated hydrocarbons through gas chromatography or mass spec chromatography(Lisec et al., 2006 . You identify carbonate pesticides through either mass spec or HPLC (high-performance liquid chromatography (Matuszewski et al.., 2003), a technique in analytical chemistry used to separate, identify, and quantify each component in a mixture. It relies on pumps to pass a pressurized liquid solvent containing the sample mixture through a column filled with a solid adsorbent material.

Mildew, Mold and Fungus

Mildew, mold, and fungus (bacteria) can be identified through a microscope and don't need mass spectrometry. If you want to identify solvents, the cannabis plant uses extracted concentrates of cannabis to formulate hash oil, wax, butter, and other forms. Extraction can take place involving solvents through several different methods including carbon dioxide, butane, propane, ethanol, isopropyl alcohol, acetone, and other solvents.

For health and safety purposes, a solvent must be removed from the final product before consumption. It's not good for the human body. Residual solvent concentrations can be measured with gas chromatography and flame ionization detection. States do not have any mandated guidelines, but at an international level, led by the International Council of Harmonization (ICHO), provides guidelines for understanding the necessarily levels of residual solvents (Kumkumian, 1994).

Heavy Metals

Lastly, heavy metals can be tested through ICP or mass spectrometry analysis. Heavy metals include lead, mercury, arsenic, cadmium, chromium, as well as others. These are largely monitored and regulated by the Food and Drug Administration (FDA).

Note: when it comes to total THC and total CBD, the equation for total THC is actually THC+THCA, and the equation for total CBD is measured as the sum of CBD and CBDA.

What Goes into a Certificate of Analysis?

It is important that we navigate our data journey with an understanding of what a Certificate of Analysis is, because along the way we can think about this data pipeline and how regulation is likely to take hold. Every individual plant will receive a bar code number that it can be tracked with from seed-to-sale. A Certificate of Analysis is the minimum number of likely tests to be performed and tracked along this data pipeline. The first component that is important for a Certificate of Analysis is the client sample ID. Each medical manifest will probably have a unique lot number for traceability, as well as notes about the origin company and facility.

Second, is the description of the different tests involved in the analysis. Typically, this will include bacterial counts, but is actually likely to be three different types of tests. One will involve living things and heavy metal contaminants as previously discussed. The second is the cannabinoid profile, which involves the psychoactive and less psychoactive elements. And then, the terpene or terpenoid profile, as a test description. In a Certificate of Analysis, you'll find a method reference. The typical methods that might be involved in the process are reported as well. In each reporting, we use a tolerance limit. This could involve the tolerance for medical and chemical analysis. The different units used for different types of analysis are:

- aerobic bacteria count as CFU/g (Colony Forming Unit per gram)
- bile tolerance as MPN/g (Most Probable Number per gram)
- aflatoxins as N/g (or Nanograms per gram)
- heavy metals as Mg/Kg (or milligrams per kilogram)

Microwave Digestion

Microwave digestion and cold vapor analysis are used to define the cannabinoid profile. The method reference typically used is called OAS-SV21. This is the recommended method for the identification and analysis of cannabis and cannabis products, according to the United Nations Office on Drugs and Crime. There's no tolerance limit, but the unit is percentage for weight. The important thing to note about the C of A Analysis is that, it is not surprising to know that the THC content is significantly lower than the THCA content. The reason why this is unsurprising is that, during this analysis, the TCHA has not been decarboxylated and converted to THC. Similarly, terpenes or terpenoids, can be profiled using a method reference of OASSV23 (or the GC-MSD Testing). The tolerance limit is typically mandated and regulated by the FDA.

Getting into the terpene profile, looking at these 255 strains in our public data sample for the Open Cannabis Project, can be revealing. The Open Cannabis Project is one of the first data sources to publicly disclose the C of A analysis of different samples that have been submitted. In this product, you'll find that initially we looked at water percentage, which has a minimum of zero and a maximum of 17%, with an average of 9.97%. The standard deviation was 1.68%. The total THC content percentage that we expect is between 0 and 40%. The average among the 255 strains is 172%, with a standard deviation of 74.9%. The D9 THC content is about, on average, 4.1%, with a max of 34%, and a minimum of zero. The THCA content is 173% on average, with a lower and upper bound similar to that of total TCH. That is because this analysis accounts for the fact that THCA can be converted. The average total CBD level is about 20% vs. CBDA which is 21%. Data consistency is indicative of the current ability to perform these analysis.

Speaking to the *universe of data*, we should include other product experiences which are designated by different companies in the industry. These experiences include potential *categorical variables* like: energy, focus, uplifting, calming, sleep, pain management, anti-inflammatory and sexual vigor. As far as flavor profiles, a standard way of categorizing is sweet, berry, spicy, orange, sour, citrus, minty, herbal, mild to cooling, nutmeg, and clove. The list used in this research is important when understanding how we can categorize and create a finite closed form dataset of different profiles. This analysis and this information will be critical in performing trials and surveys that can be standardized across the industry in the future.

The Retail Market Consumer Segmentation

Segmenting the consumer market accurately is important in an industry. As long as the scope of market segmentation is *mutually exclusive and collectively exhaustive*, such that each person in that market has one favorable option, the analysis of your market or customer base will be more accurate.

Currently, there are six primary consumer archetypes within the dispensary environment that relate to consumption and spending behavior ("Cannabis Consumer Report", 2019).

However customer segments are divided into categorical variables, there are several factors that should be considered when subdividing segments.

- Age Group, which addresses the messaging and cultural acclimation that a customer segment may have received.
- Income level, which speaks to disposable spending power.
- Acceptor versus Incumbent, which speaks to whether the customer is new or old to the market.
- Loyalty, which speaks to whether a particular segment is likely to return to their last business transaction.

Brand Selection Drivers

What are the overall top brand drivers at selection? Reasonable prices, a good selection of products, and an informative, friendly staff. In relation to the acceptor segments above, affluent families appreciate having resources to support their lifestyles in daily activity and health. Baby boomers value perception, staying informed and searching for a good deal before purchasing. Frequent shoppers value the tangible qualities, lifestyle association and approachable pricing.

Opportunities for Business Growth

What are the top opportunities for business growth according to Local IQ? There is low awareness and education around the industry amongst the consumer segment. According to The Knowledge Gap, one in three people didn't even know whether their state was legal or not. Knowledge of brands and product differentiation is low. Over time, we have an increased opportunity to analyze consumer behavior (as affected by federal and state regulations), in the context of legalization in the United States and around the world.

There are currently no extreme market leaders, so brands are pressured to compete for choice and trust.

• In the United States, 67% of consumers surveyed visited two or more dispensaries in the past three months;
• Trust drives is an important factor in making brand decisions;
• Consumers adopt the brands that satisfy their immediate needs

Retail Software

For retail (POS), the industry has tracking systems (software) that can help with restocking and supply. Sometimes these softwares are combined with auto scheduling, real time inventory management, and other tools, to drive daily efficiency. In the retail environment, we have an opportunity to auto schedule for strains and specific tasks.

For example: Imagine having a strain-specific recipe database, establishing standards for future baseline grows, keeping track of nutrient timing and environmental conditions for peak performance. This can all be tracked by RFID or barcode.

Customer Feedback

Gathering insights from consumers about the products that they purchase and the experiences they have with these products is critical to innovation and development in the industry. Retailers and brands need to receive feedback in order to deliver products that meet the needs of consumers. Chat bots and automatic phone services help to facilitate this and are starting to become more prevalent throughout the industry. *Recurrent Neural Networks*, or RNNs, can be used to evaluate text in web processes automatically (Lai et al., 2015). The key is to design smart feedback systems. It's also very important to use *web scraping* to look for places where people did not complain directly to the company, but instead, posted their issues to an outside platform. Some of these platforms are monitored closely by the FDA and lead to investigations, based on information shared.

Dispensary and Comparable Analysis

The dispensary is the modern storefront for the cannabis consumer. This is where consumers have the option to walk into a physical location to inquire about and evaluate different products using their intuition and senses The evolving environment from bodega to something resembling an Apple Store, like with Med Men, creates a lot of new opportunities for measurement, analysis and prediction within the dispensary. Below we will look at the analytics of dispensary, and apply a mathematical framework for dissecting the space where much of the industry revenue is generated.

What types of analysis should be done between dispensaries? A comparable analysis is a way of measuring the value of a business, entity or process, by comparing it with businesses that share similar characteristics. For example, if you want to estimate the value of a McDonald's Franchise, you may want to compare its value to similar franchises in the area, like the Burger King next door or the Arbys in the town neighboring town.

How do we measure dispensary success?

Revenue per square foot

Revenue per employee/budtender

Customer traffic, number of customers per week

Effectivity, retail conversion rate, this is nuanced, because currently in cannabis dispensaries the effectivity rate is nearly 100% because more dispensaries either only let those who pre-order online to attend the store, or customers need to get through so many hoops to get access, like get a medicinal license, that when they arrive they are almost certain to buy. Consumers do not yet have the option of just walking into a dispensary for browsing

Average Sale, speaks to the types of customers you attract in the door on average

Items per purchase, speaks to your inventory management and the type of products you promote

Gross margin, speaks to salespersons abilities

How do we measure dispensary costs?

Price per square foot of space, fixed cost investment

Price per square foot of space, operating cost

Cost per employee hour

How do we segment dispensaries? The answer is in the previous section, which is by customer segment.

Employee Experience

The employee experience is a critical factor in understanding the consumer experience, because the employees are the point people for the transaction. How do you measure an employee's experience, and evaluate their ability to serve the consumer and the organization?

Do they have industry training or skills they have internally and externally acquired? Examples of internal training include education about the different strains, their biochemical composition and their projected effects. Examples of external training include certification that may be required by law. For example, cultivators may be required in states to be trained in "Track and trace" systems, so the employee knows how to assign a tag to each plans so it can be tracked from cultivation to retail.

How long have the been a budtender? This can be measured as both, *internal experience* and *external experience*. The cannabis industry is unique because most of the employees gained much of their experiential knowledge outside of a dispensary, well before cannabis was considered legal in their state. Thus, when measuring employee experience in trying to value the human capital in your organization, you need to ask for both internal and external experience.

Customer Service

As the markets tend to saturate with vendors, customer service and retention will become important to the growth of any business.

What are the limitations of customer service? The limitations to customer service are only limited by the amount of data you can collect on your clients. Information can be collected by either asking the consumer directly, or by incentivizing them, like through through loyalty and rewards programs.

How is customer service measured?

Before the sale point: First Response time and how long

did the customer wait before being served?

During the sale point: how many questions are asked by the customer? How many of those questions were answered to the satisfaction of the customer? Was the consumer success-fully upsold during the course of the sale? What was the average price of their transaction?

After the sale point: customer retention and how often they repurchase over a point in time? What is the Net Promoter Score, which measures the likelihood that a customer will refer you to someone else?

Environmental Design & Corporate Social Responsibility

Environmental design and Corporate Social Responsibility (CSR) are two ways that organizations can be socially account-able to their employees, their shareholders and to the public (Burke et al., 1996). Companies can achieve CSR and environ-mental goals either by setting internal targets, or adhere to new frameworks, like the B-Corp Certification, help to measure a company's social and environmental sustainability (Certifica-tion, 2019). In either case, organizations have the opportunity to allocate resources to missions that are not only considered socially good, but may be good for long-term business as well. In fact, many CSR projects are easier to justify when they are viewed as long-run investments in infrastructure and brand, in-stead of short-run projects.

Repurposing real estate for cannabis industry uses, like using abandoned warehouses to set up grow houses, has several CSR benefits. First, it saves on the environmental costs of building new structures. Second, it may reactive properties in neighbor-hoods that have not received as much business investment in recent years. Third, it saves in the financial investment of build-ing a brand new building, and may even be offset by tax breaks from government hoping to stimulate the local economy.

Environmental design also finding its way directly in the cannabis industry. One example of technologies used to further environmentally conscious design are hybrid cultivation systems. These systems use both light from the sun and from light bulbs so that they can save on electricity. Hybrid systems may also use rain water to supplement irrigation for crops.

How are we able to measure the success of CSR investments? CSR can be measured both by *objective internal results* and by *subjective external results*. Measuring *objective internal results* means looking at benchmarks like how many gallons of water have you saved or kWh of electricity from before. These measures can be scientifically measured, adjusted and improved. They can also be reported as an absolute dollar value of savings or reductions in costs. Measuring subjective external results means looking outside the organization to ask consumers, stakeholders and potential clients how they feel about the companies CSR actions. This might involve a survey of customers, and looking at relative measures like competitiveness in the industry, and how consumers feel their CSR projects measure up to comparable industry players.

Boutique, Retail, Online

Each of these methods of selling can be captured by a categorical variable. They are defined by how personal an interaction the customer receives from the store. Boutique is defined as a store where every budtender is assigned to exactly individual consumer at a time. Retail is defined as having more than one consumer on average assigned to a budtender. Online is where no budtender is assigned to directly service a consumer's purchase experience.

Consumer Insights, sub-segmentation and physical responses

Cannabis is a unique product when it comes to how a data scientist may think about the consumers relationship to the active ingredient. For example, alcoholic beverages that range from Wine to Whiskey, may have different concentrations of active ingredient and have different prices, but the active ingredient for both Wine and Whiskey is the same, ethanol. Once that ethanol is absorbed from either delivery system (Wine or Whiskey), the net effect is the same, you feel intoxicated and slightly disoriented. However, with cannabis the delivery system appears to impact the reported effects of the strain. In fact, a consumer that is ingesting a specific strain a specific THC and biochemical content but is ingesting them through two different delivery methods, like combusting flower versus vaping oil, might report completely different effects. Thus, *sub-segmentation* is an important factor when analyzing cannabis products, because the biochemical makeup of the product is not sufficient to understand the effect and experience on the consumer.

PART 4: INNOVATION AND PREDICTING THE FUTURE: WHAT DO MANAGERS NEED TO KNOW ABOUT DATA SCIENCE IN THE CANNABIS ECONOMY?

"How do we predict the future or change factors in the present to model the outcomes we want?"

Prescriptive after descriptive. Part 3 was entirely about Descriptive Methods, ways of measuring what is directly available in the present and performing basic analysis. Part 4 is about Prescriptive Methods, and asks how do we predict the future or change factors in the present to model the outcomes we want?

Introducing The Technologies Driving the Future

"These concepts combined are what provide the technological ecosystem that is enabling this new field of economics and emerging way of thinking about businesses strategically, resulting in markets with memory."

What Does GPU Mean?

Why is talking about GPU's the important first step of this section? Because GPUs, or Graphical Processing Units, are a special type of processor that is allowing data to be processed faster than ever before and the data science teams usually use that to implement advanced computational models, enabling everything from artificial intelligence modeling to calculations for the blockchain. A GPU has historically been known as the processor on your gaming graphics card. However, it was realized that the same types of calculations that are used in video games are also used in calculating machine learning models. It also means that Nvidia video cards and their GPUs involved are able to process big data analysis in the context of machine learning and artificial intelligence more quickly than a regular CPU or computer processing unit.

The CEO of Nvidia is considered a visionary, largely because Nvidia got ahead of the industry by encouraging Nvidia to create a distributed software package that enabled open source developers to utilize their technology for more than just graphics. Everything from artificial intelligence and machine learning algorithms to blockchain processing and bitcoin mining have been enabled in the last decade because of advancements in this type of computational research (Lindholm et al., 2008).

What Does IoT Mean?

Advances in the Internet of Things (IoT) have greatly enabled the big data revolution, especially within the cannabis industry. IoT is a term that was coined about two decades ago and the foundation for my first patents as a researcher at MIT. It is a concept describing how appliances or every devices can be connected to the Internet of things, becoming part of an integral network of everything in your home that can respond or be customized to create a data-rich environment. This is where your tastes as a consumer and your needs would be most closely met and satisfied.

My original three patents in the IoT space involved what we'll call a "vertical stack of technology" that is still being utilized today in many parts of the industry. The first part is in security and transmission where most of the secure technology over the Internet is performed through what we call "public key encryption", which has been used primarily through RSA or popularized by RSA, a firm in Boston. These concepts combined are what provide the technological ecosystem that is enabling this new field of economics and emerging way of thinking about businesses strategically, resulting in markets with memory.

Universal Identifying Codes (Tagging)

Tagging is an important technology and has major implications for the industry. For example, with IoT, tagging data is very helpful because it can tell you where, when and how the data came from, since the number of source appliances can be enormous and might include appliances in the future that haven't even been considered yet. Tagging currently takes many popular forms. Geotagging is where you might tag a photo with coordinates so you know where the photo was taken. Datetime tagging is where you tag a photo with the date and time when it was taken. RFID tagging (or Radio Frequency Identification) are commonly used on physical goods, like a box containing a product that is being shipped. By tagging a box that is being shipped, you might be able to know everything about the boxes journey and contents, by just reading the RFID tag with a scanning device.

When tagging anything there are important policy and technological considerations to make. First and foremost is privacy. Since the tag might contain information that is sensitive, you may want to make sure that the information is encrypted or coded in such a way that not everyone can see it. For example, if you take a picture of your house to post to Twitter, and it was Geotagged without you realizing it, then you may have just let the entire internet know about where you live. Second is deciding what information you're going to share with everyone who has access to reading the tag. In the case of the cannabis industry, it might be important for a wholesaler and retailer to know what crop the product was sourced from, because it can speak to the security of the product as well as its quality and origins. The grower may not want to include trade secret information, however, like what the inputs to the crop were, or the price they sold it at. Additionally, they may want only some parts of the supply chain to know about some aspects of the data, while keeping some of the data secret from others. For example, the grower may not want the wholesaler or retailer to know the ingredients to their crop, but they may want a laboratory testing their product to know. Using public key encryption technologies (like RSA mentioned before) or blockchain technology, this will open up opportunities for data to be shared and will build up trust along the supply chain among parties that are doing business together.

Statistical Significance

Statistical significance is the likelihood that an event did not occur by accident. For example, we quite often hear about studies that report an analysis that is at a 95% statistical significance level. This means that, on average, there is a 95% chance what you are observing is not due to chance or randomness, and is actually because of the hypothesis being tested. Statistical significance is also related conversely to the *p-value*. If the statistical significance threshold of a study is 95% or 0.95, that means the p-value is 0.05. This means that for a given feature in the model, if the p-value is set the 0.05, the parameter has at most a 5% chance on average of rejecting the original (null) hypothesis, when that hypothesis is actually true. In statistics, it is common to hear the term *p-hacking*, which refers to analysts who modify their data and their models in enough ways that their results are deemed statistically significant, even though they did not perform any extra data collection or investigation.

Market Analysis and Paralysis

When performing a market analysis, the most important question to ask is: "what is the metric in the market that we are analyzing?" This may seem obvious but there are subtle details about this question that reveal a lot about what your analysis might tell you. For example, if you can clearly define your metric, you analysis becomes easier and more informative. This is an important lesson that both decision makers and data scientists forget all the time: by preparing the guidelines for your analysis upfront, you can avoid what we affectionately call "paralysis by analysis". Paralysis by analysis is what happens when you do not state upfront what you're looking for, and you keep trying to attack the problem from a different angle when the analysis doesn't answer the question exactly how you asked. While it may seem like a noble idea to keep analyzing something until you discover something, what happens more often than not is that we don't end up finding more answer, but rather we tweak how we explain the analysis and our explanatory variables in order to get closer to our desired result.

This is called *endogeneity*, and should be avoided at all costs. Endogeneity broadly refers to situations in which an explanatory variable is correlated with the error term. Similarly, we want to avoid *confounding variables* as they occur when some variable or factor ends up affecting our model even if we don't measure it directly.

Vertical vs. Horizontal Integration

Vertical integration and horizontal integration are the two axes through which you can look at market segmentation and the supply chain. A way of looking at the industry from a vertically integrated axis is to look at the market from top to bottom, or from seed to sale. A vertically integrated company is one that grows its own plants, harvests and processes them into retail packaging, and then sells the packaged product directly to the consumer. It is easy to think of the vertical axis in the vertical integration model as time, with rising as we go through the supply chain. There are also varying degrees of vertical integration. A company doesn't need to operate all the way from seed to sale to have elements of vertical integration. A company that creates its own seeds, and then grows those seeds into plants is still *partially vertically integrated.*

Similarly, horizontal integration is where you look at the industry from a particular snapshot in time or common place in the supply chain. For example, if growers in the industry were required by law to get all of their seeds from a single source, like the government, then the seed supply for the industry would be considered horizontally integrated.

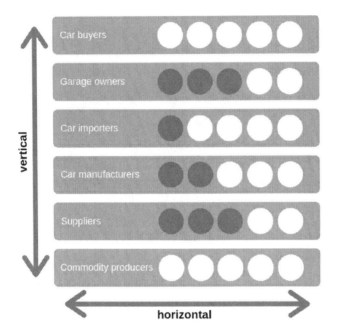

Illustration of Integrations using example of the Automotive Industry.

Information Asymmetry and the Integrity of Data

Information asymmetry is the study of understanding decisions when information between parties is either incomplete or unequal. The truth is that everywhere in life, just like everywhere in business or along a data pipeline, it is hard for all parties to have all of the information. Sometimes it is not important to have complete information, but in those situations where information is complete, it can affect the outcome of the situation. Information asymmetry is an important consideration in the cannabis industry, which leads us two two important questions: where does information asymmetry play into the cannabis industry, and what can be done about it?

Between the person who is supplying the inputs to a plant and a cultivator. Those who are supplying inputs of the fertilizer to a cultivator, know the true inputs to the fertilizer, while the cultivator may not actually know what has gone into the product. In order to reduce information asymmetry here, legal requirements for standardized and thoroughly descriptive labeling are important. Additionally, it is not uncommon for products in new markets to meet *short-run standards*, like passing a test of chemical requirements of a fertilizer, but failing to meet *long-run standards*, like making sure that those chemical requirements continue to pass, even though the fertilizer stays on the shelf for a couple years. Since we are dealing with a new market, most of these discoveries only happen once the industry has a fully matured supply chain in which these types of issues get observed by multiple parties along the way and fixed. They are difficult to predict; however, studying supply chain breakdowns in other comparable industries, like agriculture or food production, may serve as a starting point and important benchmarks in a predictive model.

Information asymmetry exists between the cultivator and the wholesaler. The wholesaler is receiving a packaged product from the cultivator, but the wholesaler does not necessarily know if the product and strains received are exactly what were promised. To help solve this, state mandated track and trace systems that track the source of the plant material from the cultivator down the supply chain are helpful. Also, implementing the use of standardized testing kits across the industry will also be critical. Currently, there does not exist an industry standard for testing; this may be an important means of reducing information asymmetry in the future.

Testing standardization and kits will also help to reduce information asymmetry between wholesalers and dispensaries, as well as give consumers the power to test their own products. Another example of the difference between the short-run versus long-run standard was in the ingredients for vape cartridges. In the short-run, the ingredients did not appear to have any issues, and vaping was largely considered to be the less damaging alternative to combustion-based smoking. In 2019, however, reports of deaths from long-run vaping due to contamination from Vitamin E Acetate in the vaping solution revealed an information asymmetry that could not be observed in the short-run.

Transparency and Reproducibility

The foundation of all science is transparency and reproducibility. If scientific results cannot be explained transparently, then people will not believe them. If the results are not reproducible, then people will not believe them. This is true of any model you create. If you are not transparent about the inputs, it will make your model difficult to document and even harder to use. If the results are not reproducible, then nobody is going to believe you model in the first place.

Data Aggregation and Data Engineering

In order to manage all the data that is coming into your system, it is important to understand the role of data engineering. *Data engineering* is an often misunderstood term that is often combined with data science. Data engineering and data science are related in that they both deal with data, however they are completely different roles within an organization. Data engineering is the role of making sure your company has the hardware, software and infrastructure tools for collecting, storing and securing data. Data engineers are also responsible for making sure that the data is stored in the right format, if the company is getting its data from multiple sources, that all of the data is integrated in the right way and also data is maintainable and clean and easily accessible. To oversimplify, a data engineer's job starts at the source of the data and ends once the data is cleaned (or *munged*). A data scientist's job starts where the data engineers job ends, with data that can be organized and analysis to provide insights to the business. That is not to say that the roles can't overlap, however, more often than not, I have observed that managers within organizations often have misconceptions about the data roles they are trying to create on their team, which can lead to poor leadership and misused resources.

Regression modeling

Regression modeling is what you learned in grade-school algebra: drawing a line on a graph through data points. Regression modeling is what is commonly used in Microsoft Excel. A regression model takes inputs, and measures the average effect on the output. The model measures a distance between a line and each data point and finds the best line to minimize the distance of that line and data points. Then when we provide the new data point input using the lines formula, it calculates (predicts) an estimate for the output. To do this, you need input and output data to train your regression model.

Model *calibration* means to use training data (typically historical data) to figure out what the *parameters* of the equation are. Model calibration or tuning is using not only training data but also other numerical methods to make sure that the model behaves in a certain criteria, like with high accuracy given the training data. The *parameters* of the equation are the values that are given to the average effects measured by the model. Parameters are the values that control the size of the behavior of the model. Parameters tell the model how to behave in order to find the optimal or best answer. For example, y=mx+b is a classic regression model, with m and b being the parameters.

Training Data, Cross Validation and Testing Data

When you want to train your model, you will need data and a way to know if you've trained your model well. The industry standard for doing this is to take a data set, and split it into two sets: a training dataset and a testing data set. The proportion between these two is typically 80% and 20% respectively. This means that you train your model with 80% of your available data, and you set aside the other 20% to see how accurate your model is at predicting new results. If you make the mistake of training you model on 100% of the data, and then test it on some 20% of the data, then you will be fooling yourself into believing your model is more accurate than it is, because you will be testing the model on data it has already seen. This is the equivalent of giving a student a history exam two times in a row, and then using the second score to judge whether the knew what they were talking about in the first place.

Cross validation is another option for helping tune your model. *Cross validation* is when you resample and test your model against different algorithm options to decide if the model you're using is actually the best one. It typically happens between the initial training of the model and the final testing of the model. If you want to perform cross-validation as part of your model training regimen, then it is common to split your data 60% for training, 20% for cross validation and 20% for testing.

Supervised Learning

Supervised learning is a type of machine learning model that assumes you start with some background knowledge with how the data is structured. Having background knowledge of the model typically means three things. First, we are comfortable making assumptions about the shape the model will take. Typically the more assumptions you make, the easier it is to program and faster to run a model, but you sometimes trade away accuracy. Second, you are able to train the model based on having a set of both input and output values you trust to calibrate the model. Third, you know whether the data is taking the form of *numerical* data or *categorical* data. Numerical data is the data that is in the form of numbers, like 1, 2, 3.5, etc.. Categorical data is data that is the form of categories, like dog, cat, cheese, high, low, etc.

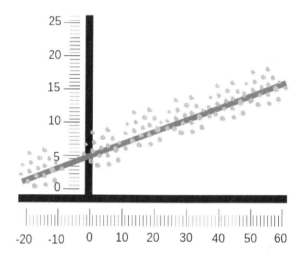

Illustration of Regression Function.

The two major forms of supervised learning are regression and classification. Regression analysis is just like what you learned in grade-school algebra: you draw a line of best fit to go through points on a graph. It is actually a form of supervised learning. Another example of a Supervised Machine Learning Model is referred to as a "Classification model". Classification models are where you want to sort a bunch of objects into groups by classifying them. With classification problems, you know what types of differences you are looking for, which can make sorting easier. An example of a classification problem is to train a model to look at images of fruit and tell you what type of fruit it is. Another application for supervised learning is using image detection to decide if a cannabis plant has fully flowered yet, or if there is a disease on the leaf. By training the model with images of leaves that we know have diseases versus ones that don't, we can feed in new pictures to ask whether or not the leaf pictured has a disease or not.

To do a quick dive into the breadth of supervised learning out there, here is a brief list of other models you might hear about. Logistic regression is like Linear regression, but instead of the line we are accustomed to seeing in Linear regression, logistic regression typically gives a probability somewhere between 0 and 1. If the value is closer to 1, you classify the object as a 1; if the value is closer to 0, you classify the object as a 0.

Another model is the decision tree. The decision tree, instead of a list of variables, returns a list of rules, where you can classify data.

Another common supervised learning model is known as the Nearest Neighbors. This means that instead of classifying something as either "A or B", or "0 or 1", we can provide a basket of data points, and let the model decide how to fit them into groups. Then, we decide which the new data point is closest to which one of the previous ones, then based on that it predict the new data points for us.

Unsupervised Learning

Unsupervised learning is slightly more tricky than tricky than supervised learning, because you're making fewer if any upfront assumptions about the data you're given. This means you don't know how the outputs might relate to the inputs or how the inputs relate to each other, but you do have input data.

Unsupervised learning is often a good first step when performing research and exploratory analysis, especially if you know very little about what you're studying and looking for a starting point. There are two main ways that unsupervised learning is applied.

First, a concept called "clustering". Clustering is when you throw all the data at the model, and ask the model to sort the data into X number of groups based on metric we defined. For example, let us say we have geolocation points and we want to cluster them into three groups that are closest together. So here, our metric is distance. We use clustering methods to find three groups of points that are closest together using the distance metric. Thus if you ask your clustering algorithm to sort the model into 3 groups A, B or C, then your output will be three lists that contain each data point tagged as either being likely part of group A, B or C. This does not inherently mean that groups A, B or C describe anything, that is up to the data scientist to apply logic, interpret the results and explain them. Decision makers can also offer their business acumen to see if the groupings make logical sense. However, if you're not sure how different parts of your data are related, this may be a great starting point to figuring out the features of you data. The brain does a great job of clustering all the time, and is easy to see this process in children who are learning. Let's say you're looking at images of animals, but were learning about animals for the very first time. You may not know that animals with 4 legs typically walk on the ground, and that animals with long flat arms can fly. However, you do know enough to separate them into two groups by looking at their images. After you have them separated into two groups, then you can ask more questions about what makes them seperate unique groups.

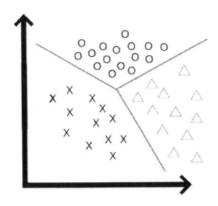

Illustration of clustering in machine learning.

Second, is dimensionality reduction. Dimensionality reduction is typically applied through an algorithm called PCA or Principal Component Analysis. PCA is an example of "hierarchical clustering", which means that you are not only clustering, but you're clustering to see what combinations of factors might be the most important. For example, just by what you've read in this book, there may be more than a hundred inputs that go into how a cannabis plant grows. However, since creating a model takes time and resources, you aren't interested in all 100 inputs, and instead you want what combinations of features explain the variable in your model in less feature space. By running a PCA model, you can see which factors have the most impact on the whole system as well as other factors (Ramaseshan, 2013).

Recommendation System and Content Delivery

Recommendation systems are ways of targeting content delivery to users based on observable user behavior and past user behavior that can be saved as data. They are everywhere on the internet now, from Netflix suggesting your next TV show to binge, to Amazon, where they advertise directly to you products that you might be interested in buying. They are typically a combination of supervised and unsupervised learning techniques. When thinking about designing a recommendation engine, I would encourage you to consider 3 important factors upfront:

1. What data can we collect from our users?
2. What kind of algorithm do we want for our recommendation engine?
3. How do we measure the success of our recommendation system?

Each of these answers depend on each other. To illustrate this thought process, let us walk through a case study. For example, if we are designing an algorithm for recommending cannabis strains to user, we can start by asking, what data can we collect from the user. Data collection might be as basic as the cashier asking a question at the time of checkout, or a feedback form that the user can fill out with an iPhone app. If we have a single question, like "did you enjoy the strain: yes or no?" the answer to questions #2, which algorithm to use, is also pretty straight forward. You may use one of the classification algorithms discussed above.

Now, how do we measure the success of the recommendation system (#3)? The answer to this question isn't as obvious as it seems. Intuition might tell us to check to see if our sales went up after implementing it. However, the success of the recommendation engine is not based on whether or not sales went up. It is the fact of whether or not the user accepted the recommendation. Sales going up can be dependent on many other factors such as delivery of the recommendation or the message.

Now what if we want to make a more sophisticated recommendation system. First, we must start with the data we are able to collect. Let us say we are able to collect information from consumers about what strains they enjoy consuming, as well as the delivery mechanism through which the consumer ingests the product (vaporizer, edibles, flower, etc). The second question will become slightly more challenging, because one algorithm may not be enough to give an accurate recommendation. For example, you may use a classification algorithm first to see what strains they tend to buy the most, and then use a regression model to guess which strains they might enjoy based on terpene and cannabinoid profiles. To then see if you recommendation system was a success, you can check to see not only if sales went up, but also if the consumer ends up buying the recommended strain for multiple visits thereafter.

Reinforcement Learning

Reinforcement learning is the closest thing we have to artificial intelligence, and is the closest machine learning analogy to training a rat to run through a maze. Instead of training a computer model based on data you already have from an environment you've already been studying, reinforcement learning learning takes a slightly different approach, in that it provides the model with an environment and a set of reward rules, and let's the model start to explore. Beyond that, not only does the model explore, but the model will measure its decisions and the effects of its decision in the future. Basically it weighs all of the decisions and their impacts of decisions based on the previous decisions, and charts the next step in its path. Everytime the model takes an action in the environment that we want to reinforce, then we reward the model with a higher score. If the model takes an action that we don't want to reinforce, then we punish the model with a lower score for taking that action.

Applying the Technologies Driving the Future

"By orchestrating their work together correctly and efficiently, data scientists and data engineers can work together in complementarity to create and deliver models and insights to decision makers and empower organizational leaders."

Doctors

What are the Theoretical Effects of Cannabinoids and Health Benefits? How can medical professionals measure the outcomes?

CBDV is a non-psychoactive cannabinoid that is a homologue of CBD. CBDV is known for its ability to help temper nausea and vomiting and the treatment of epilepsy and other neurological issues (Burstein, 2015). It was also considered a stimulant for bones. CBD-A, as previously discussed, is one of the four results of CBGA converting into other cannabinoids. It can help as an anti-inflammatory and intestinal contractions. CBG is anti-inflammatory, anti-bacterial, anti-tumor and bone stimulant. THC-V is known to help with appetite suppression, pain relief, anti-nausea, epilepsy and anti-inflammatory (Baker, 2003). It's also being explored for weight loss, diabetes, anti-epileptics appetite suppression and Parkinson's disease. THC-A is also working as an anti-seizure and anti-inflammatory and anti-tumor. CBN is most effective in bone growth, stimulating appetite, inhibiting cancer cell growth, and combating insomnia. Again, CBC is another derivative of CBG. CBC, one of the four derivatives, is well known as being anti-bacterial, anti-fungal, and anti-inflammatory, as well as helping with cancers (Russo, 2011).

THC has a psychoactive effect, but is known to help with depression, spasms, pain, sleep apnea, and glaucoma. CBD has antidepressant, anti-anxiety, antipsychotic, anti-seizure, neuro-protective, and anti-diabetic properties.

Science can tell us a lot about the potential benefits of canna-bis, but every patient's actual experience is an individualized journey. Thus, it is important to perform a Patient Level Ana-lysis (PLA) on Medicinal Outcomes in order to understand how patients may best benefit. A survey is the traditional way of getting patient feedback about cannabis treatment, and it is important to account for as many variables as possible when designing your survey procedure and system, in order to main-tain the integrity of the data. (Bonn-Miller, 2014)

The structure of the survey is important for both getting stat-istically significant results, as well as for making sure that the surveys get filled out by patients in the first place. An important first consideration in structuring your survey is to decide how often data is to be collected. In data science, this is called the *cadence*. Currently, some doctors survey their patients only once every 6 months (about twice as often as you are recommended to get your physical), and that is able to provide them with actionable data and some statistical significance in resulting analysis. However, the cadence of data collection would benefit from being much more often than that, like monthly, as is re-quired for most Schedule 1 substances like opioids.

After deciding on cadence, collecting the data should be ano-nymized with some basic demographic information like gen-der, age, zip code and other facts collected.

Next, the survey questions should be structured in such a way as to help the patient report what may turn out to be the trans-formational effects of the treatment. The survey can be meas-ured on a scale, typically 1 to 10 in order to provide enough resolution for analysis, as well as a set of categorical variables mentioned below. A combination of objective and subjective data are recommended since most of what is treated by cannabis and its alternatives are actually symptoms, not causes -- which is why the subjective, self-reported nature of the data is actually helpful. These questions include:

-How long have you been a patient?

-What condition are you seeking treatment for? This may be a categorical variable that includes:

Anxiety, Chronic Pain, Glaucoma, Musculoskeletal spasticity, Migraines, Multiple Sclerosis. Intractable epilepsy, Amyotrophic lateral sclerosis, Terminal Cancer, Tourette's Syndrome, PTSD, IBS/Crohn's Disease, Terminal illness, Seizure disorder, Cancer, Muscular Dystrophy, HIV/AIDS.

-What symptoms do you find medical cannabis helps you with?

Appetite Energy, Neuropathy, Mood, Depression & Anxiety, Chronic pain, Headaches, Muscle Spasms, Arthritis, Sleep.

-What are your methods of medicating that you prefer?

-What if any side effects with cannabis treatment have you experienced?

-Which dispensaries do you prefer?

-What are your preferred strains?

-How many times a day do you medicate?

-How is your pain level today on a scale?

-After starting the medical cannabis program, what medications have you been able to reduce or completely stop? If so, please describe what medicine you have been able to reduce.

-Has your level of energy and activity level changed since starting the program?

-How satisfied are you with the service you received by the medical professionals administering your treatment?

-Would you recommend a medical marijuana program to other patients with your condition?

-Has medical cannabis improved your quality of life?

In February 2019, the results of my study on patient outcomes was presented at the CannaTech Conference. The study of over 9000 surveys of patients revealed a statistically significant drop in the usage of opioids among patients who had received medical education and prescriptions for cannabis. These results are reflected in other studies including a decade-long study that found that states with medical marijuana programs saw significantly lower numbers of opioid related overdoses between the years 1999-2010 (Bachhuber, 2014). Math saves lives.

Data Infrastructure

Data infrastructure is critical when it comes to the cannabis industry because so much of the data is health related. When designing data infrastructure, there are three important types of data to consider:

"Data at Rest" refers to data that is physically stored in a hard drive or in the cloud and is not being moved anywhere. It can be patient records or sales histories. It is desirable for data at rest to be encrypted, but depending on the type of database or storage technology you are using, the database may not have encryption at rest available. For example, Amazon Web Services had previously offered a Relational Database System (RDS like PostGres of MySQL) with encryption a year before if offered the same for its Non Relational Database Systems (like MongoDB).

"Data in Motion" is data that is moving across a network. It is important here to watch for hackers and those who are "sniffing" the network for packets of data to intercept. Technologies like RSA are used to help protect data in motion, the same encryption technology to protect your credit card transactions over the internet. This is also known as public key encryption.

"Data in Use" is data that is currently being changed, processed or analysed. Security measures here involve access permissions and managing credentials for those who have authority to access the data.

ETL versus ELT

Creating a pipeline to take in your data and make it usable is a critical step in creating a sustainable data infrastructure for your company. ETL is the most common way of thinking of data pipelines in 3 steps: Extract, Transform and Load. This means the data is extracted from a source, like a website or a table of values; it is then transformed into a structure that is compatible with your system, and then loaded into your data warehouse. From the data warehouse, data scientists can then query the database and build models that can reveal business insights.

More recently, with advances in cloud computing and storage capabilities, the next generation of processes are being done in industry at ELT instead of ETL. ELT changes the order of pipeline operations to Extract, Load, then Transform. The idea of Loading before Transforming means, that you Load your data right away into your data warehouse, or what we now refer to as a *data lake*. Since cloud computing technology enables access to nearly limitless amounts of storage and computing power, data does not need to be pre-processed into a standard structure, like a relational database, to be useful for later use. Data lakes are spaces in the cloud where you can store large amounts of data in the raw form and then when you're ready to create business insights and perform analytics, you can then transform the data in that last step into a form that best suits your processing needs. Data lakes and ELT are advantageous in a world where we are being bombarded by new and different types of data every day, because there is no requirement that the data need to fit a certain structure before being loaded into the system.

Producing models: the dance between data science and data engineering

A model is simply defined as a series of mathematical instructions that help to answer a question. Whenever starting a project, we always start with a question. For example, we can look at our retail sales data for a dispensary and ask the question, *what demographic factors about clients tell us whether they are more likely to buy flower or vape cartridges?* A data scientist will then take this question and start researching the available *features*, or data points, that can help us answer this question. A data scientist needs to first consider not just what data is available, but also the policy issues behind how they can use the data. For example, it is important that a data scientist know when data is deemed private and that any identifying information must be removed. Additionally, the data scientist must also be aware of how that data is being used, like ensuring that the demographic data was voluntarily provided and is not being used to discriminate between consumers, but rather is being used to enhance the average consumers experience. Other factors a data scientist must consider may include: what type of mathematical model is required to solve this problem? Are there any software packages or frameworks we can use to help solve this problem? What assumptions does the model need to make in order to get to the most efficient result? What are the tradeoffs between accuracy and precision we are interested in making in the model? What are some basic performance metrics we need to have in place so we know the model is making material improvements that will affect the business positively? The model is then prototyped into a *minimum viable product,* or MVP, which provides a series of results, or an output table of results, that can be tested during *Quality Assessment*, or QA, by those who want to make sure that the MVP reflects the desired business logic as well as performance thresholds desired by decision makers.

Once the MVP is completed in the development environment and passes QA, it is handed from the data scientist to a data engineer, who will then convert it into the production system. The production system is where the final code that analysts and decision makers can use gets stored to be able to get results from. Data engineers are responsible for making sure the model is converted and coded in such a way that it fits into the system and can answer questions from those who need the insights. They ask questions like: how fast do answers need to be delivered to the decision makers and what engineering tradeoffs do we need to make in order to do that? How much storage and computational power do we need in our system or cloud service to let this model run effectively? What unit tests do we need to create to make sure the model is working consistently and effectively across the system?

By orchestrating their work together correctly and efficiently, data scientists and data engineers can work together in complementarity to create and deliver models and insights to decision makers and empower organizational leaders.

Opioid Crisis and Substitution Models

According to the National Institute on Drug Abuse, on average, over 130 people die everyday of opioid overdoses everyday in the United States. There are a few ways that analysis and machine learning have already been used to help fight the opioid epidemic.

Spatial analysis of how consumers receive their medical products can indicate whether they are at risk of being addicted to the product and abusing it. A spatial analysis is when we use geographic coordinates in order to understand the behavior of

187

the system. For example, by tracking where opioids are being distributed, machine learning algorithms like support vector regressions can help us see where on a map there is an unusually high concentration of opioid prescriptions, like at the borders between states (Cepeda et al., 2013). This might indicate that consumers are crossing state lines in order to receive their prescriptions from different doctors to double their supply of drugs.

Substitution Models are another important option. A *substitution model* is where you give the consumer two different options that achieve the same level of satisfaction. For example, a consumer who has been using opioids may find that a cannabis strain with a 20:1 CBD to THC ratio help them to reduce their opioid intake. Looking at the first order effect, or direct effect, as the person continues to substitute cannabis products with different cannabinoid-terpene profiles for their opioids, they incrementally achieve the same feeling while consuming less opioids. To dig deeper and into *second order effects*, or reinforcing effects, we may find that not only are they consuming less opioids, but they also do not need as strong a dosage of the CBD or cannabis in order to continue reducing their intake of opioids.

International Expansion and The Possibilities of technology

Access to technology is critical to the empowerment of industry across the world, especially the rising economic powers in Africa. In fact, laws implemented by African countries in the 1900s made cultivating the plant only attractive to the resource-poor farmers (Duvall, 2019). However, for an industry to thrive, incentives and infrastructure must be in place for a diverse set of decision makers to act, not just the resource-poor farmers. Incentives and policies are already changing on the African continent. With the decreasing cost of infrastructure,

McKinsey Director Acha Leke asserts that "technology firms in Africa must navigate some big infrastructure challenges – including the fact that internet data is still significantly slower and more expensive in Africa than on other continents" (Leke and Sibanda, 2019).

Public Health Analysis

When it comes to performing a public health analysis, new models and ways of thinking are required to address potential future issues. For example, due to incomplete and flawed analysis, cannabis was categorized as a Schedule 1 Substance for having no "accepted medical use" and for having a "high potential for abuse" (and addiction). Updates in public health policy, data collection and analytical methods are necessary for making sure that future public health analysis adequately protects and empowers the consumer.

Public health policy needs to pivot to allow governmental and non-governmental bodies to work together to develop studies. By withholding funding or erecting barriers between research institutions, public health measures will impair the ability for studies and analysis to take place. Like in all organizations, the ability to create actionable results between decision makers and data scientists requires requires transparency which leads to the ability to share and synthesize ideas. For example, advocating for substances to be designated as Schedule III instead of Schedule I, make it much easier for researchers to get access to the drugs for study. Organizations like MAPS, the Multidisciplinary Association for Psychedelic Studies, and its founder Dr. Rick Doblin, have been advocating for similar reforms since the 1980s (Doblin, 2002).

Data collection for public health analysis is important to determine measurable outcomes. If the correct data is not being collected, you are not going to be able to correctly measure the effect you're looking for. A 2010 NIH study found that the current analytical tools for measuring addiction propensity and severity were lacking (Conway et al., 2011). Additionally, new types of data are becoming available that will shed light on addiction and the effects of drugs on individuals, through widespred genetic testing of consumers.

Public health policy can also benefit with rethinking what analytical methods are best used for answering a question. For example, just performing a measurement of blood composition is not sufficient for seeing if there is any impairment to driving a motor vehicle after consuming cannabis, while it may be sufficient to measure blood alcohol level (Sewell et al., 2009). An NIH study found that understanding impairment needed a model that measured not just physical factors but also psychological factors about the subject, in order for researchers to understand that there were multiple dimensions of factors, including behavioral compensation, that as allowing for drivers intoxicated with cannabis to appear more capable of driving than those who are alcohol intoxicated.

Randomized Control Trials

Randomized Control Trials (RCTs) are a method of testing the effect of an intervention by randomly dividing the group into two sets and testing to see if the treatment has a statistically significant impact (Duflo & Kremer, 2005). On a personal note, Esther Duflo a pioneer in the field, was one of my economics professors and one of the first people to inspire me, teaching me that I could use my memory and hyperthymesia in a way to advance research. RCTs has been a critical tool for studying the impact of policies in the developing world, where a natural experiment may not explicitly exist but there are opportunities to create one. For example, if a school is opening in a new village, just by knowing in advance that a new school is opening gives researchers the opportunity to set up an experiment to observe the effects of that school's opening on the community.

For example, this could be seen in observing crime rates before and after the school opens, such that the results might reveal a relationship between the two. When researchers and implementers work more closely together, there are opportunities to observe and study the effects of policy interventions as if it is nearly a natural experiment.

The concept of RCTs may prove as invaluable in the implementation of cannabis in developed markets, as it does for poverty alleviation studies in the developing world. Explicit testing of the effects of cannabis on individuals has historically been difficult for researchers to get authorizations. However, since decriminalization and legalization being implemented in different states are America at different times and in different ways, therein lies an opportunity for policymakers and researchers to implement RCT like studies in order to advance the understanding of changing policies in the space of cannabis and other drugs.

Predicting De-stigmatization and Behavior Changes of Consumers

Cultural factors can have just as large an impact on consumer preferences as the quality of the product itself. For example, the stigma associated with cannabis, through historical terms like "weed" and "ganga", may turn off consumers who find negative feelings in those stigmas. These stigmas also affect the total possible cannabis market size. According to Marshall Ogen, Vice President of Business Strategy for CannabisBPO, even terms like "recreational use" have become so deeply associated with the battles for legalization, that policy makers and industry leaders are now advocating for the term "personal use" in order to de-stigmatize it. The changes often start with how the laws themselves are written and the language behind new laws and policies can have a powerful effect on consumer behavior. By performing an event driven analysis over time, we can see whether or not there is a measurable impact on consumer behavior.

Dosing and Time Series Analysis

Time series analysis is about looking for effects that happen over time. It is commonly used in financial models and extends to the event driven analysis mentioned above. However, one of the most important uses of time series analysis when it comes to advances in machine learning and measuring biochemical feedback is with dosing.

Understanding and predicting the effects of dosing are important to the industry from both a medical and personal use standpoint.

When it comes to medical research, it is important to know exactly how much of a substance is required to achieve a certain positive health outcome. Since it is nearly impossible to overdose on cannabis, this means that cannabis can be prescribed by just allowing the person to start consuming, instead of mandating a maximum threshold of consumption, like with opioids (Greene, 2019). However, this does not mean you need to smoke enough to get stoned to feel a medical benefit. Much smaller doses might allow for medical benefits without impairing the consumer. However, the time delay in absorption caused by different delivery methods means that it is hard to track how dosing leads to different effects on the consumer.

Currently there are few technologies that allow for dosing, but that is quickly changing. One of Time Magazine's "25 Best Inventions of 2016" was actually a vape pen by Dosist, that would administer a certain amount of mg of THC or CBD (TIME Staff, 2016). More companies are research not just mechanical ways of dosing, but creating compounds that help time the release of edibles into your bloodstream through digestion. Beverage manufacturers are looking at opportunities to get THC into the bloodstream more quickly, which may help facilitate the rise of "bud bars", or bars that provide cannabis, similar to existing wine bars. Since consumers do not need to wait for more than a few minutes to start feeling the effects of alcohol, it is possible to enjoy wine at a bar in a way that cannot yet be done with cannabis. Machine learning models that engage with consumers in experiential settings like a "bud bar" may provide real-time feedback to the consumer and allow them to achieve the feeling they want.

Brand Impact and Naming Conventions

Is the name of the strain or the biochemical makeup more important to average rating that a consumer gives to a strain? In order to answer this question, I collected data on all 2,832 strains of cannabis registered with Leafly, and joined those datasets with other public data sets to get a better understanding.

The first insight of interest is that THC concentration is not actually a statistically significant feature affecting the average rating that reviewers gave a strain. In fact, the only of the cannabinoids or terpenes that had any remotely significant effect was guaiol (p-value less than 0.15), which has a strong scent of cypress pine associated with it.

The second insight is that medicinal-users appear to be more critical during their strain reviews than personal-users. This seems reasonable since they may have received more education about the product just by going through the process of getting a medical card.

Lastly, the strain type (sativa, indica or hybrid) does have a statistically significant effect on average rating. However, the effects between sativa and indica were nearly identical, they were a full standard deviation greater than the effect of hybrids. In order words, people tend to favor non-hybrid strains on average more than hybrid strains.

Network Effects and Measuring
Digital Marketing Impacts

A *network effect*, also known as demand side economies of scale, are the effects we observe on the overall value of a system whenever we add one additional person or customer to that system. A basic example of a network effect is the bandwagon effect, where when we see an additional person joining a cause, we are more likely to join as well, creating a *positive feedback loop* (Shapiro, 1998).

The dependent variable is *awareness level,* a metric that measures the amount of digital traffic that a certain name or concept is receiving. This can be measured through analytics and tracking software. For this study, Google Trend data was used as a proxy. To measure the *relative initial capital,* built up by each person a comparable analysis is performed also using Google Trends to evaluate if someone has a relatively high, low or none initial social capital associated with a subject. For example, Calvin Broadus Jr. (aka the rapper Snoop Dogg), spent much of his documented career advocating and speaking about cannabis, so he can be said to have built up a large amount of capital before ever making a digitally recognized statement associated with cannabis. On the other hand, Robert Gronkowski spent most of his NFL career not speaking about his relationship to cannabis, until after his retirement, where he then launched a relationship with a CBD company.

The *event function* represents the relationship of the person to the effect, which can take the form of either an impulse function or a step function. An *impulse function* is a function that has value at only one point in time. This is analogous to a one time event involving a person with no subsequent follow up, like when a celebrity posts a picture of themselves smoking cannabis and does not then post again in any regular interval.

A step function, as mentioned in previous sections, involves a sudden step up, and then maintains that higher level, like when someone endorses a cannabis product and stays involved with the company.

To measure a *first-order impact*, you can search the trend in direct association with the person's name. To measure a *second-order impact*, you can observe when an event occurred for the first-person and measure the awareness increase of the second-person party.

While there are many examples of different network effects, I have highlighted a few in this section.

The Robert Gronkowski Effect: Zero Initial Capital, Event Driven Impulse Function, First Order Effect, when professional capital from one business is used to promote social capital in another. For most of his career, Gronkowski spoke little about his relationship to CBD, until he announced his partnership with CBDMedic. After the announcement, we see a spike in awareness and a quadratic decrease toward a steady state level of awareness.

The Seth Rogen Effect: Zero Initial Capital, Event Driven Step Function, First Order Effect. In June of 2008, the advertising campaign for Pineapple Express, a movie about cannabis consumption, was preparing for the release of the film later that summer. This marked the beginning of many projects by Seth Rogen in the space of cannabis, including launching a cannabis brand in March of 2019. The step function represents his ability to raise awareness in the space via the release of a consistent body of work and involvement in the industry.

The Calvin Broadus Jr. Effect: Significant Initial Capital, Event Driven Step Function, First Order Effect, where a degree of social capital accumulated in a pre-legitimized market is suddenly monetized within a legitimized market. His appearance on the cover of Blender Magazine in January of 2005 marks one of the biggest increases in awareness in the cannabis space that has not been matched by any private figure, until Gronkowski announced his partnership above.

One lesson in the above three cases is that in order for awareness to be sustained, those who are mediums for awareness need to incorporate it into their long-term professional or personal narrative. This makes sense from the perspective of network effects, because a person can speak once, but their professional and their personal narrative can continue to speak on their behalf into the future. Additionally, both Rogen and Broadus started raising awareness for cannabis before the era of big data, which may have given them an anchored position in the measurement of awareness across time. Gronkowski, on the other hand, has now entered the space already occupied by incumbents, and his experience of maintaining interest in his product over time may involve more investment in the awareness he is bringing to the market.

Below are two examples to demonstrate the difference between first-order and second-order impacts. Although only one explicitly deals with cannabis, they still help to illustrate the difference.

The Stefani Germanotta Effect: Non-Zero Initial Capital, Event Driven Impulse Function, First Order Effect. Germanotta (aka the performance artist Lady Gaga) had accumulated some initial social capital in the cannabis space by being outspoken about how she involves it in her life and work. However, in November 2012 the awareness she brought to the cannabis space increased by nearly 7 times, when she posted a picture of herself dressed at Halloween in a cannabis dress. Her ability to invoke such awareness by placing her own personal name on the line is a demonstration of a powerful first order effect.

The Taylor Swift Effect: Non-Zero Initial Capital, Event Driven Step Function, Second Order Effect. Taylor Swift is a supporter of the LGBTQ community. In one instance, she did not tell people explicitly to donate to the advocacy organization known as GLAAD, however, she did include an indirect mention in one of her song lyrics. The result of including a mention in her lyrics of her album was a noticeable uptick in donations to the organization. "The fact that she continues to use her platform and music to support the LGBTQ community ... is a true sign of being an ally" said Anthony Ramos, director of talent engagement at GLAAD.

Ultimately, education and awareness are empowerment, and cross collaborations that capitalize on network effects will become more common in the future. Filmmaker Spike Jonze collaborated with dispensary company MedMen to produce a short film educating the public about the origins of the hemp plant and that it was grown by President George Washington himself (Jonze, 2019). Professionals in all spaces are using their voices to help advance awareness and education.

Visual Analysis of Flower and Convolutional Neural Networks

Performing a visual analysis on the flower has a range of machine learning applications in the cannabis industry. A common machine learning algorithm used in visual analysis is known as a Convolutional Neural Network (CNN). A CNN (not related to convolutional markets), as an algorithm that use layers of perceptrons (digital representations that are coded to work like the neurons in the human brain) to try to understand an image. They are also known as *feed-forward neural networks*, because the processing of data only goes in one direction from start to finish, and does not feedback. Unlike RNNs discussed below, CNNs are also not dependent on time or order, which is why they are good at image processing, which involves a snapshot in time or a moment.

For example, if you give a CNN an image of birds flying through the air, you may want to ask the algorithm to count the numbers of birds in the image. If the CNN has three layers, the first layer might look at the most obvious contrasts in the image, like between the white colors of the birds against the blue sky. Let's say after this first layer of "perceptrons" that the image see 10 white objects in the sky that could be birds. That does not mean that all 10 candidate objects are birds. The second layer of perceptrons may look more closely to see if the white objects have a shape similar to what we might expect as birds. This may narrow down our total possible bird count from 10 to 8. The third layer of perceptrons then looks at the white objects that are shaped like birds, and then looks at the texture of the objects to see if the texture of the objects matches what we might expect to see in a birds feathers. In this step, we find that of our 8 remaining candidates, only 5 were actually birds, while 3 were eliminated as clouds. Thus, our CNN is able to identify 5 birds in the sky.

Instead of performing an analysis of birds, smartphone apps and other image processing technology can be used to take pictures of cannabis leaves, to address everything from plant maturity during the grow process to diagnosing plant diseases. Nutritional deficiencies in the plant soil can also be observed by visual changes in the leaf, and can be automated through video monitoring of crops. CNNs are not restricted in their use to image processing, and their computing power can also be used in other machine learning applications, like recommendation systems.

Customer Feedback and Recurrent Neural Networks

Collecting and analyzing customer feedback is an important way in identifying and serving their needs. Often times customer feedback is collected in the form of written comments. These comments can be analyzed for factors, like keyword frequency, sentiment, tone and positivity. While keyword frequency is straightforward to measure, you can simply count the words in a sentence, understanding sentiment is much more challenging, which is why we introduce the concept of Recurrent Neural Networks (RNNs) to perform this analysis. RNNs are good for answering questions that are time and order dependent, like understanding the sentiment behind a sentence. The reason why RNNs are time and order dependent is because in order to understand what a sentence means, you need to break it down into its parts of speech, and in order to best understand what was being said at the end of the sentence, you need to remember who was mentioned as the subject at the beginning of the sentence. RNNs go through a process similar to CNNS with layers of perceptrons, but a RNN allows data to be feedback into the previous perceptrons, making it ideal of language processing or even speech processing.

Online Retail and the Future of Cannabis Commerce

Due to the fact that cannabis is still illegal at the Federal level, most online cannabis retail in the United States is restricted to paraphernalia, equipment and *ancillary services*, or services that do not touch the plant product itself. Companies like A Pot For Pot have developed clever methods of selling grow kits online, without selling the plant itself. However, when legalization eventually occurs at the Federal level and there is no longer an issue of interstate commerce, companies will want to collect as much data about their consumers as possible through their online portals. Currently, there are many ways of collecting data about the consumer, like with seeing what types of products they put in their shopping cart, and how many they actually purchase in the end. However, new technologies and network models are helping reveal not just what consumers are purchasing, but also how they are reaching those purchasing decisions. For example, by tracking the links on a website that a consumer clicks on before they make their purchase, we can see how the directional model representing their thought process behind their purchase. Does the consumer go directly to the product purchase pages, or do they also click on the links about product education as well? With new web technologies and *full-stack development* that links the front-end to the back-end of the website as one system, we can even track the consumers mouse as they navigate the website to learn about the consumer behavior and experience.

As the availability of technologies increase and the cost of computing power decreases, the opportunities for application of machine learning models to serve the consumer are as limitless as the human imagination.

Acknowledgements

I want to extend my deepest gratitude to several individuals who have played a role in the creation of this journey and this research endeavor. So many of my colleagues, friends and family have shared a piece of themselves through their support and their intellect and their time.

Rich Greene for your support, public policy expertise, and patience through the editing process. Shahin Taghikhani for your wisdom in the space of data science, for your insights into the editing of this book. Thomas Mazzuchi for your advisement and for standing up for your students, Melda Buyukozturk for your brilliance and editorial insight, Jacque Peacock for your knowledge and wisdom, Kristen Downs for your tireless patience and editorship, Bennett Hillenbrand and Cori Lynne Fleser for your insights, Victor Christopher Cabral for your patience and belief in my ability to develop software, Arnaub Chatterjee, Karen Attiah for her support and friendship through this process, Dan Berman, Marshall Ogen, Zahir Dossa, Elvira Stalteri, Denise Garland, Bryan Bryson, Oren Karev, Ally Peverly, Joshua Mezher, Mo Darwazah, Sirene Abou-Chakra, Ben Bowers, Thong Nguyen, Ben Droz, Rhamey Said, Eduardo Mclean, Beri Meric, Dhruva Rajendra, Cody Pope, Aaron Sobel, Farhad Agharahimi, Jason Levin, Evan Clinthorne, Amanda Nguyen, Anjana Mohan, Jay Ravani, Julian Cohen, Aaron Chadbourne, Laura Bassett, Hannah Rappleye, Seth Collins, Zachary Ozer, Omar Darwazah, Gary Su, Yoav Cohen, Jane Harris, Greg Palmer, Dani Stouck, Cole Corey, Duncan Miller, Avi Margolies, David Lallemant, Brian Weiner, Kat and Daley, Jeffrey Sachs, Dan and Moah Gardella, Peter Pitts, Craig Binkley, Bruce Newman, Eli Clark-David, Radha Agrawal, Scott Hartley, Alira, Alex and Henry Morstadt, Amit Mukherjee, Raja Palaniappan, Linus Bloomqvist, Jessica Lovering, Andy Goldfarb, Lars Plate, Douglas Holt, Sian Griffiths, David Rice, Rachel Lindsey, Robert Leke, Isabel Celeste, Rosy Khalife and Paul

Tyan, Connor Twyman, Sam Brinton, Ricky Ramsaran, Will Carpenter, Behrooz Afghahi, Tim Patch, Tessa Velázquez, Evan Foster, James Emery, Nicola Scandiffio, Abrima Erwaih, Scott Rudder, Mark Wien, Joseph Nucci, Bob Miglani, Nicki Lehrer and Mauricio Paredes, Robert Solow, Noah Berman, Bonaventure Ngu, Hillary Vagg, Jessica Harpole, Pierre-Andre Chiappori, Satyajit Bose, Ezgi Hacisuleyman, Chris Coleman, Nicholas Hinrichsen, Kameron Winters, Moon Javaid, Eric Dementhon, Charlotte Clymer, Gary L.S. Allen, Adam Goers, Eric Lubell, Julie Stenberg, Chris Gerling, Kyle Hendrick, Eleni Valasis, Wendy Wen, Aniva Hinduja, Robert Haferd, Austin Gallegher, Brian Keegan, Lindy Snyder, Jackie Beer, Giselle Sorial, Kelley Detweiler, John Guttag, Dorothy Curtis, Chris Meeusen, Maher Nader, Sam Brinton, Frances Rogoz, David Autor, Esther Duflo, Duncan Anderson, Thomas Hay, Layla Khani, Sandy Simmons, and Julia Kardon who unknowingly through her patience and wisdom guided me through finishing this book, so that I could be prepared to write the book I was meant to write in the first place. Thank everyone for their patience with a book designed to intentionally bend the readers mind through its novel structure and reflection of the view. Omeed Veiseh for his support and my whole family. Finally, to Sholeh and Merdad Veiseh, the two best parents that fortune could bring to a young mind.

WORKS CITED

Abelseth, Brian. "Blockchain Tracking and Cannabis Regulation: Developing a Permissioned Blockchain Network to Track Canada's Cannabis Supply Chain." *Dalhousie Journal of Interdisciplinary Management*, 2018, ojs.library.dal.ca/djim/article/view/7869.

Abrahamsson, Pekka, et al. "Agile Software Development Methods." *VTT*, 2002, www.vtt.fi/inf/pdf/publications/2002/P478.pdf.

Abrams, Donald I., et al. "Vaporization as a smokeless cannabis delivery system: a pilot study." Clinical Pharmacology & Therapeutics 82.5, 2007.

Acemoglu, Daron, Simon Johnson, and James A. Robinson. "Institutions as a fundamental cause of long-run growth." Handbook of economic growth 1, 2005.

Altman, Naomi, and Martin Krzywinski. "Points of Significance: Association, correlation and causation.", 2015.

Anderson, Jeffrey E, et al. "The Highs and Lows of the Cannabis Industry: A Pestle Analysis of the Current Issues." *Cal State LA*, 2019, www.calstatela.edu/sites/default/files/groups/College%20of%20Business%20and%20Economics/PDF/business_forum_27_vol_2_full.pdf#page=27.

Applied Engineering in Agriculture, vol. 16, no. 5, 2000, pp. 505–508., doi:10.13031/2013.5301.

Arrow, Kenneth Joseph; Arnott, Richard J.; Atkinson, Anthony A.; Drèze, Jacques (editors) (1997). Public Economics: Selected

Papers by William Vickrey. Cambridge, UK: Cambridge University Press.

Atakan, Zerrin. "Cannabis, a Complex Plant: Different Compounds and Different Effects on Individuals." *Therapeutic Advances in Psychopharmacology*, 2012, journals.sagepub.com/doi/full/10.1177/2045125312457586.

Bachhuber, Marcus A., et al. "Medical cannabis laws and opioid analgesic overdose mortality in the United States, 1999-2010." JAMA internal medicine 174.10 (2014): 1668-1673.

Baker, David, et al. "The therapeutic potential of cannabis." The Lancet Neurology 2.5 (2003): 291-298.

Baron, Anat. "The Future IS Cannabis." MJBizCon NEXT, June 2019, New Orleans, LA. Keynote Address.

Bascietto, John, et al. "Ecotoxicity and Ecological Risk Assessment. Regulatory Applications at EPA. Part 1." *Environmental Science Technology*, 1990, doi:10.1021/es00071a001.

Bassani, Marina, et al. "Humidity Stress Responses in Pollen of Anemophilous and Entomophilous Species." *Taylor & Francis Online*, 2009, www.tandfonline.com/doi/abs/10.1080/00173139409428991.

Baye, Michael R. *Managerial Economics and Business Standards*. McGraw Hill-Irwin, 2014.

Beck, Kent, et al. "Manifesto for agile software development." (2001): 2006.

Ben-Shabat, Shimon, et al. "An entourage effect: inactive endogenous fatty acid glycerol esters enhance 2-arachidonoyl-glycerol cannabinoid activity." European journal of pharmacology 353.1, 1998.

Benowitza, Neal L., and Jack E. Henningfield. "Nicotine Reduction Strategy: State of the Science and Challenges to Tobacco Control Policy and FDA Tobacco Product Regulation." *Prevent-*

ive Medicine, Academic Press, 23 June 2018, www.sciencedirect.com/science/article/pii/S0091743518302019.

Berinato, Scott. "Data Science and the Art of Persuasion." *Harvard Business Review*, 16 Jan. 2019, hbr.org/2019/01/data-science-and-the-art-of-persuasion.

Berthold, Wolf, and Ralph Kempken. "Interaction of Cell Culture with Downstream Purification: a Case Study." *SpringerLink*, Springer, Dordrecht, 1 Jan. 1994, link.springer.com/chapter/10.1007/978-94-011-0257-5_26.

Birur, Dileep K., Thomas W. Hertel, and Wallace E. Tyner. "The biofuels boom: implications for world food markets." The Food Economy Global Issues and Challenges. Wageningen, Wageningen Academic Publishers, 2009.

Bohn, T., et al. "Chlorophyll-Bound Magnesium in Commonly Consumed Vegetables and Fruits: Relevance to Magnesium Nutrition." *Wiley Online Library*, John Wiley and Sons, Ltd (10.1111), 31 May 2006, onlinelibrary.wiley.com/doi/abs/10.1111/j.1365-2621.2004.tb09947.x.

Bócsa, I., P. Máthé, and L. Hangyel. "Effect of nitrogen on tetrahydrocannabinol (THC) content in hemp (Cannabis sativa L.) leaves at different positions." J Int Hemp Assoc 4 (1997): 80-81.

Bonn-Miller, Marcel O., et al. "Self-reported cannabis use characteristics, patterns and helpfulness among medical cannabis users." The American journal of drug and alcohol abuse 40.1 (2014): 23-30.

Brinton, W. C. (1914). Graphic Methods for Presenting Facts. United States: The Engineering Magazine Company.

Brunings, Asha M., et al. "Are phosphorous and phosphoric acids equal phosphorous sources for plant growth." IFAS Extension. Horticultural Sciences Department, Univ. of Florida 1 (2012).

Burke, Lee, and Jeanne M. Logsdon. "How corporate social responsibility pays off." Long range planning 29.4 , 1996.

Burns, John Edward, and Jin-Su Kang. "Comparative economic analysis of supporting policies for residential solar PV in the United States: Solar Renewable Energy Credit (SREC) potential." Energy Policy 44, 2012.

Burstein, Sumner. "Cannabidiol (CBD) and its analogs: a review of their effects on inflammation." Bioorganic & medicinal chemistry 23.7 (2015): 1377-1385.

"Cannabis Nursery Ordinance." *City of Berkeley*, 2017, www.cityofberkeley.info/uploadedFiles/Planning_and_Development/Level_3_-_Commissions/Commission_for_Medical_Cannabis/Pappas_NURS-ORD-LIC_final.pdf.

Cannabis Tech. "What Does Hemp Biomass Actually Mean?" *Cannabis Tech*, 2018, www.cannabistech.com/webcasts/ask-a-hempster/what-does-hemp-biomass-actually-mean-cannabis.

CDC. "Outbreak of Lung Injury Associated with E-Cigarette Use, or Vaping." *Centers for Disease Control and Prevention*, Centers for Disease Control and Prevention, 2019, www.cdc.gov/tobacco/basic_information/e-cigarettes/severe-lung-disease.html.

Cepeda, M. Soledad, et al. "Distance traveled and frequency of interstate opioid dispensing in opioid shoppers and nonshoppers." The Journal of Pain 14.10, 2013.

"Certification." *Certification | Certified B Corporation*, 2019, bcorporation.net/certification.

CFSAN. "Three GRAS Notices for Hemp Seed-Derived Ingredients for Food." *U.S. Food and Drug Administration*, FDA, 2018, www.fda.gov/food/cfsan-constituent-updates/fda-responds-three-gras-notices-hemp-seed-derived-ingredients-use-human-food.

Chan, Gary C.K., et al. "User Characteristics and Effect Profile of Butane Hash Oil: An Extremely High-Potency Cannabis Concentrate." *Drug and Alcohol Dependence*, Elsevier, 8 June 2017, www.sciencedirect.com/science/article/abs/pii/ S0376871617302557.

Chandra, Suman, et al. "Cannabis Cultivation: Methodological Issues for Obtaining Medical-Grade Product." *ScienceDirect*, Academic Press, 13 Feb. 2017, www.sciencedirect.com/science/article/abs/pii/S1525505016305881.

Chang, Hoshing. "Research Gaps Related to the Environmental Impacts of Electronic Cigarettes." *Tobacco Control*, BMJ Publishing Group Ltd, 1 May 2014, tobaccocontrol.bmj.com/content/23/suppl_2/ii54.

Church, James C., and Mahmoud A. El Sohly. "Changes in Cannabis Potency Over the Last 2 Decades (1995–2014): Analysis of Current Data in the United States." *Science Direct*, Elsevier, 19 Jan. 2016, www.sciencedirect.com/science/article/abs/pii/ S0006322316000457.

"Climate Change: The IPCC Scientific Assessment." Edited by J.T. Houghton et al., *Repositorio CCT CONICET-CENPAT*, 1990, repositorio.cenpat-conicet.gob.ar:8081/xmlui/bitstream/handle/123456789/497/climateChange.pdf?sequence=1.

Colombo, Claudio, et al. "Review on Iron Availability in Soil: Interaction of Fe Minerals, Plants, and Microbes." *SpringerLink*, Springer Berlin Heidelberg, 30 Nov. 2013, link.springer.com/article/10.1007/s11368-013-0814-z.

Combinator, Y. "Q&A With Zahir Dossa, Cofounder of Function of Beauty." *Y Combinator*, 11 Oct. 2018, blog.ycombinator.com/ qa-with-zahir-dossa-cofounder-of-function-of-beauty/.

Comer, James. "H.R.5485 - 115th Congress (2017-2018): Hemp Farming Act of 2018." *Congress.gov*, 12 Apr. 2018, www.congress.gov/bill/115th-congress/house-bill/5485.

Crosby, Michael, et al. "Blockchain technology: Beyond bitcoin." Applied Innovation 2.6-10, 2016.

Da Porto, C., D. Decorti, and F. Tubaro. "Fatty acid composition and oxidation stability of hemp (Cannabis sativa L.) seed oil extracted by supercritical carbon dioxide." Industrial Crops and Products 36.1, 2012.

De Klerk, Geert-Jan, Jolanda Ter Brugge, and Svetla Marinova. "Effectiveness of indoleacetic acid, indolebutyric acid and naphthaleneacetic acid during adventitious root formation in vitro in Malus 'Jork 9'." Plant cell, tissue and organ culture 49.1, 1997.

de Meijer, Etienne PM, and L. J. M. Van Soest. "The CPRO Cannabis germplasm collection." Euphytica 62.3, 1992.

Dixon, Robert O.D., and Christopher T. Wheeler. "Biochemical, Physiological and Environmental Aspects of Symbiotic Nitrogen Fixation." *SpringerLink*, Springer, Dordrecht, 1 Jan. 1983, link.springer.com/chapter/10.1007/978-94-009-6878-3_5.

Doblin, Rick. "A clinical plan for MDMA (Ecstasy) in the treatment of posttraumatic stress disorder (PTSD): partnering with the FDA." Journal of psychoactive drugs 34., 2002.

Duffy, Daniel. "The Liquor Control Act and Liquor Prices." *THE LIQUOR CONTROL ACT AND LIQUOR PRICES*, 2009, www.cga.ct.gov/2009/rpt/2009-R-0278.htm.

Duflo, Esther, and Michael Kremer. "Use of randomization in the evaluation of development effectiveness." Evaluating development effectiveness 7, 2005.

Dussy, Franz, et al. "Isolation of Δ9-THCA-A from Hemp and Analytical Aspects Concerning the Determination of Δ9-THC in Cannabis Products." *Forensic Science International*, Elsevier, 18 Aug. 2004, www.sciencedirect.com/science/article/pii/S0379073804003408.

Duvall, Chris S. "A Brief Agricultural History of Cannabis in Africa, from Prehistory..." *EchoGéo*, Pôle De Recherche Pour L'organisation Et La Diffusion De L'information Géographique (CNRS UMR 8586), 13 July 2019, journals.openedition.org/

echogeo/17599.

EPA. "Summary of the Federal Insecticide, Fungicide, and Ro-denticide Act." *EPA*, Environmental Protection Agency, 15 Aug. 2019, www.epa.gov/laws-regulations/summary-federal-insecticide-fungicide-and-rodenticide-act.

Elzinga, S, et al. "Cannabinoids and Terpenes as Chemotaxo-nomic Markers in Cannabis." *My Best Bud CA*, 2015, mybestbud-ca.com/wp-content/uploads/cannabinoids-and-terpenes-as-chemotaxonomic-markers-in-cannabis-2329-6836-1000181.pdf.

Fawcett, J, and EL Buhle. "Using the Internet for Data Collection. An Innovative Electronic Strategy." *Europe PMC*, 1 Jan. 1995, europepmc.org/abstract/med/8529140.

Gleichmann, Nicole. "Cannabis Sativa Vs Indica: Is There a Difference?" *Analytical Cannabis*, July 2019, www.analyt-icalcannabis.com/articles/cannabis-sativa-vs-indica-is-there-a-difference-311780.

Google Patents. "US20080229657A1 - System and Methods for Continuous Biomass Processing." *Google Patents*, Google, 0AD, patents.google.com/patent/US20080229657A1/en.

Greene, Tristan. "Coroner Claims Woman Overdosed on Can-nabis, Scientists Call Bullshit." *The Next Web*, 7 June 2019, thenextweb.com/insights/2019/06/07/coroner-claims-woman-overdosed-on-cannabis-scientists-call-bullshit/.

Harari, Yuval Noah. Homo Deus: A brief history of tomorrow. Random House, 2016.

Hawkesford, Malcolm, et al. "Functions of Macronutrients." *ScienceDirect*, Academic Press, 19 Aug. 2011, www.sciencedirect.com/science/article/pii/B9780123849052000066.

Highsmith, Jim, and Alistair Cockburn. "Agile software develop-ment: The business of innovation." Computer 34.9, 2001.

Hilderbrand, R L. "Hemp and Cannabidiol: What Is a Medicine?" *NCBI*, Journal of the Missouri State Medical Association, 2018, www.ncbi.nlm.nih.gov/pmc/articles/PMC6140266/.

Hillig, Karl W. "Genetic evidence for speciation in Cannabis (Cannabaceae)." Genetic Resources and Crop Evolution 52.2, 2005.

Hillig, K.W. "Genet Resour Crop Evol." *SpringerLink*, Kluwer Academic Publishers, 2003, doi.org/10.1007/s10722-003-4452-y.

Hudak, John. "The Farm Bill, Hemp Legalization and the Status of CBD: An Explainer." *Brookings*, Brookings, 13 Dec. 2018, www.brookings.edu/blog/fixgov/2018/12/14/the-farm-bill-hemp-and-cbd-explainer/.

Janischewsky, D.E. Proceedings Saratov II(2):14-15, 1924.

Jonze, Spike, director. *The New Normal. YouTube*, 2019, www.youtube.com/watch?v=g74sc4O8vqg&feature=youtu.be.

Kahneman, Daniel, and Amos Tversky. "Prospect theory: An analysis of decision under risk." Econometrica 47.2, 1979.

Krugman, Paul. "Increasing returns and economic geography." Journal of political economy 99.3 (1991): 483-499.

Kumkumian, Charles S. "International Council for Harmonization Stability Guidelines: Food and Drug Administration Regulatory Perspective - Charles S. Kumkumian, 1994." *SAGE Journals*, 1994, journals.sagepub.com/doi/abs/10.1177/009286159402800301.

Lai, Siwei, et al. "Recurrent convolutional neural networks for text classification." Twenty-ninth AAAI conference on artificial intelligence. 2015.

Leafly. Public Dataset, 2019, http://www.leafly.com.

Leke, Acha, and Tawanda Sibanda. "Why Africa's Digital Boom Is Only Just Getting Started." *World Economic Forum*, 2019, www.weforum.org/agenda/2019/09/why-africas-digital-boom-is-only-just-getting-started/.

Li HL, Lin H. An archaeological and historical account of cannabis in China. Econ Bot., 1974.

Lindholm, Erik, et al. "NVIDIA Tesla: A Unified Graphics and Computing Architecture ." *IEEE.org*, IEEE, 2008, ieeexplore.ieee.org/abstract/document/4523358.

Lisec, Jan, et al. "Gas Chromatography Mass Spectrometry–Based Metabolite Profiling in Plants." *Nature News*, Nature Publishing Group, 27 June 2006, www.nature.com/articles/nprot.2006.59.

Luckx, Marie, et al. "Silicon and Plants: Current Knowledge and Technological Perspectives." *Frontiers in Plant Science*, 10 Mar. 2017, www.frontiersin.org/articles/10.3389/fpls.2017.00411/full.

"The Madoff Case: A Timeline." *The Wall Street Journal*, Dow Jones & Company, 12 Mar. 2009, www.wsj.com/articles/SB112966954231272304?mod=googlenews_wsj.

Manski, Charles F. "Semiparametric Analysis of Random Effects Linear Models from Binary Panel Data." *Econometrica*, vol. 55, no. 2, 1987, pp. 357–3612., doi:10.2307/1913240.

Matuszewski, B. K., et al. "Strategies for the Assessment of Matrix Effect in Quantitative Bioanalytical Methods Based on HPLC-MS/MS." *Analytical Chemistry*, 2003, pubs.acs.org/doi/abs/10.1021/ac020361s.

McKernan, Kevin, et al. "Metagenomic Analysis of Medicinal Cannabis Samples; Pathogenic Bacteria, Toxigenic Fungi, and Beneficial Microbes Grow in Culture-Based Yeast and Mold Tests." *NIH.gov*, 7 Oct. 2016, www.ncbi.nlm.nih.gov/pmc/articles/PMC5089129.1/.

Mehmedic, Zlatko, et al. "Potency trends of Δ9-THC and other cannabinoids in confiscated cannabis preparations from 1993 to 2008." Journal of forensic sciences 55.5, 2010.

Mills, Evan. "The Carbon Footprint of Indoor Cannabis Production." *Energy Policy*, Elsevier, 16 Apr. 2012, www.sciencedirect.com/science/article/pii/S0301421512002285.

Mishra, D., and M. Kar. "Nickel in Plant Growth and Metabolism." *SpringerLink*, Springer-Verlag, 1974, link.springer.com/article/10.1007/BF02860020.

Moran, M. S., et al. "Combining the Penman-Monteith equation with measurements of surface temperature and reflectance to estimate evaporation rates of semiarid grassland." Agricultural and forest Meteorology 80.2-4, 1996.

Mowery, David C., and Timothy Simcoe. "Is the Internet a US invention?—an economic and technological history of computer networking." Research Policy 31.8-9 (2002): 1369-1387.

Munro, Sean, Kerrie L. Thomas, and Muna Abu-Shaar. "Molecular characterization of a peripheral receptor for cannabinoids." Nature 365.6441 (1993): 61.

"A Nuclear Disaster That Brought down an Empire." *The Economist*, The Economist Newspaper, 26 Apr. 2016, www.economist.com/europe/2016/04/26/a-nuclear-disaster-that-brought-down-an-empire.

Ostrom, Elinor. Governing the commons: The evolution of institutions for collective action. Cambridge university press, 1990.

Painuly, Jyoti P. "Barriers to renewable energy penetration; a framework for analysis." Renewable energy 24.1, 2001.

Pérez-Lombard, Luis, et al. "A Review of HVAC Systems Requirements in Building Energy Regulations." *Energy and Buildings*, Elsevier, 23 Oct. 2010, www.sciencedirect.com/science/article/abs/pii/S0378778810003774.

Perrotin-Brunel, Helene, et al. "Solubility of Δ9-tetrahydrocannabinol in supercritical carbon dioxide: Experiments and modeling." The Journal of Supercritical Fluids 52.1, 2010.

"Plant Shape, Sativa vs. Indica." *The Green Joint*, 2017, thegreenjoint.com/indica-vs-sativa-whats-difference/.

Potter, David J. "Cannabis horticulture." Handbook of Cannabis; Pertwee, RG, Ed.; Oxford University Press: Oxford, UK (2014): 65-88.

Priy, Surya. "Clustering in Machine Learning." *GeeksforGeeks*, 9 Feb. 2018, www.geeksforgeeks.org/clustering-in-machine-learning/.

Quora, 2019, www.quora.com/What-is-the-difference-between-normal-distribution-and-uniform-distribution.

Rahn, Bailey, et al. "The Derivation of Modern Cannabis Varieties." *Taylor and Francis*, 2016, www.tandfonline.com/doi/abs/10.1080/07352689.2016.1273626.

Rahn, Bailey. "Cannabis Anatomy: The Parts of the Plant." *Leafly*, 7 Oct. 2019, www.leafly.com/news/cannabis-101/cannabis-anatomy-the-parts-of-the-plant.

Ramaseshan, Ajay. "Figure 3." *Research Gate*, 2013, www.researchgate.net/figure/Toy-Data-in-3-dimensions-PCA-transforms-this-data-into-a-2-dimensional-representation_-fig7_259479391.

Ranalli, Paolo, and Gianpietro Venturi. "Hemp as a Raw Material for Industrial Applications." *SpringerLink*, Kluwer Academic Publishers, 2004, link.springer.com/article/10.1007/s10681-004-4749-8.

"A Revolutionary Treatise Goes on the Block." *The Economist*, The Economist Newspaper, 6 June 2019, www.economist.com/books-and-arts/2019/06/06/a-revolutionary-treatise-goes-on-the-block.

Romano, Luigi, and Amo Hazecamp. "Cannabis Oil: Chemical Evaluation of an Upcoming Cannabis-Based Medicine." *STCM*, 2013, www.stcm.ch/en/files/hazekamp_cann-oil_2013.pdf.

Romer, Paul M. "Endogenous technological change." Journal of political Economy 98.5, Part 2, 1990.

Russo, Ethan B. "Taming THC: potential cannabis synergy and phytocannabinoid-terpenoid entourage effects." British journal of pharmacology 163.7 (2011): 1344-1364.

Sacco, Lisa N. "Drug Enforcement in the United States: History, Policy, and Trends." *Fas.org*, Oct. 2014, fas.org/sgp/crs/misc/R43749.pdf.

Seifritz, W. "CO2 disposal by means of silicates." Nature 345.6275, 1990.

Sewell, R Andrew, et al. "The Effect of Cannabis Compared with Alcohol on Driving." *The American Journal on Addictions*, U.S. National Library of Medicine, 2009, www.ncbi.nlm.nih.gov/pmc/articles/PMC2722956/.

Shakespeare, William, and Helen Gray Cone. Merchant of Venice. New York, Globe School Book Co, 1900] Web.. https://lccn.loc.gov/00002890.

Shapiro, Carl, Shapiro Carl, and Hal R. Varian. Information rules: a strategic guide to the network economy. Harvard Business Press, 1998.

Sharma, Ratnesh, et al. "Water Efficiency Management in Datacenters: Metrics and Methodology." *Water Efficiency Management in Datacenters: Metrics and Methodology - IEEE Conference Publication*, IEEE, 2009, ieeexplore.ieee.org/abstract/document/5156773.

Sinek, Simon. Start With Why: How Great Leaders Inspire Everyone to Take Action. New York, N.Y.: Portfolio, 2009.

Small, Ernest. "Evolution and Classification of Cannabis Sativa (Marijuana, Hemp) in Relation to Human Utilization." *SpringerLink*, Springer US, 19 Aug. 2015, link.springer.com/article/10.1007/s12229-015-9157-3.

Small, Ernest, and David Marcus. "Hemp: a new crop with new uses for North America." Trends in new crops and new uses, 2002.

Smart, Rosanna, et al. "Variation in Cannabis Potency and Prices in a Newly Legal Market: Evidence from 30 Million Cannabis Sales in Washington State." *Wiley Online Library*, John Wiley and Sons, Ltd (10.1111), 4 July 2017, onlinelibrary.wiley.com/doi/abs/10.1111/add.13886.

Smith, Brian C., et al. "Optimization of Cannabis Grows Using Fourier Transform MidInfrared Spectroscopy." *Technology Networks*, 0AD, cdn.technologynetworks.com/tn/Resources/pdf/optimization-of-cannabis-grows-using-fourier-transform-mid-infrared-spectroscopy.pdf.

Solow, Robert M. "A contribution to the theory of economic growth." The quarterly journal of economics 70.1, 1956.

Stangler, Dane, and Robert E. Litan. "Where Will the Jobs Come From?." Available at SSRN 1580139, 2009.

"State License Types and Descriptions." *Mendocino County*, 2019, www.co.mendocino.ca.us/bos/meetings/28304/28334/28514/28551/LicenseTypes28551.pdf.

Stoll, Deborah. "The Weed-Trimming Robots Are Here." *Weedmaps News*, Weedmaps, 11 Feb. 2019, news.weedmaps.com/2019/02/the-weed-trimming-robots-are-here/.

Sun, Lena. "Contaminant Found in Marijuana Vaping Products Linked to Deadly Lung Illnesses, Tests Show." *The Washington Post*, WP Company, 7 Sept. 2019, www.washingtonpost.com/health/2019/09/05/contaminant-found-vaping-products-linked-deadly-lung-illnesses-state-federal-labs-show/.

Swartz, Mimi, and Sherron Watkins. Power failure: The inside story of the collapse of Enron. Crown Business, 2004.

Tejero, Iván Francisco García, et al. "[PDF] Impact of Plant Density and Irrigation on Yield of Hemp (Cannabis Sativa L.) in a Mediterranean Semi-Arid Environment - Semantic Scholar." , 2014.

Thien, Chih-Ching, and Ja-Chen Lin. "A Simple and High-Hiding Capacity Method for Hiding Digit-by-Digit Data in Images Based on Modulus Function." *Pattern Recognition*, Pergamon, 29 Aug. 2003, www.sciencedirect.com/science/article/abs/pii/S0031320303002218.

TIME Staff. "Inventions 2016: The Best of This Year." *Time*, Time, 2016, time.com/4572079/best-inventions-2016/.

Toonen, Marcel, Simon Ribot, and Jac Thissen. "Yield of illicit indoor cannabis cultivation in the Netherlands." Journal of Forensic Sciences 51.5 (2006): 1050-1054.

Tversky, Amos, and Daniel Kahneman. "Loss aversion in riskless choice: A reference-dependent model." The quarterly journal of economics 106.4, 1991.

Tyner, Wallace E. "Policy alternatives for the future biofuels industry." Journal of Agricultural & Food Industrial Organization 5.2, 2007.

USDA. "Industrial Hemp." *National Institute of Food and Agriculture*, 2018, nifa.usda.gov/industrial-hemp.

Veiseh, Nima. "Reconciling Acemoglu and Sachs: Geography, Institutions and Technology." Journal of International Affairs, vol. 64, no. 1, 2010, pp. 205–220. JSTOR, www.jstor.org/stable/24385195.

Wall, Matthew, et al. "Dissociable Effects of Cannabis with and without Cannabidiol on the Human Brain's Resting-State Functional Connectivity." *Journal of Psychopharmacology*, vol. 33, no. 7, 2019.

Waxman, Olivia B. "The Link Between U.S. Marijuana Law and Mexican Immigration." *Time*, Time, 20 Apr. 2019, time.com/5572691/420-marijuana-mexican-immigration/.

Weiblen, George D., et al. "Gene duplication and divergence affecting drug content in Cannabis sativa." New Phytologist 208.4, 2015.

West, Jason B., et al. "Stable Isotope Ratios of Marijuana. I. Carbon and Nitrogen Stable Isotopes Describe Growth Conditions*." *Journal of Forensic Sciences*, vol. 54, no. 1, Dec. 2008, pp. 84–89., doi:10.1111/j.1556-4029.2008.00909.x.

"Why Boveda Is Different." *Boveda® Official Site*, OAD, bovedainc.com/about-us/makes-boveda-different/.

Williamson, E. M., & Evans, F. J. Cannabinoids in clinical practice. Drugs, 60(6), 2000.

Worldbank.org. *Physicians (per 1,000 People)*. 2018, data.worldbank.org/indicator/SH.MED.PHYS.ZS.

Yang, Rayoung, and Mark W. Newman. "Learning from a Learning Thermostat: Lessons for Intelligent Systems for the Home." *ACM Digital Library*, ACM, 2013, dl.acm.org/citation.cfm?id=2493489.

Zhou, M, et al. "Services in the Cloud Computing Era: A Survey." *Services in the Cloud Computing Era: A Survey - IEEE Conference Publication*, Oct. 2010, ieeexplore.ieee.org/abstract/document/5666772.

Zikopoulos, Paul, and Chris Eaton. "Understanding Big Data: Analytics for Enterprise Class Hadoop and Streaming Data." *ACM Digital Library*, McGraw-Hill Osborne Media, 2011, dl.acm.org/citation.cfm?id=2132803.

Zuardi, Antonio Waldo. "History of cannabis as a medicine: a review." Brazilian Journal of Psychiatry, 28.2, 2006.

Made in the USA
San Bernardino, CA
07 November 2019

59402442R00129